DK EYEWITNESS BOOKS

PHOTOGRAPHY

Studio camera

Victorian photographic album

35-mm film

35-mm slides

Modern digital camera

Darkroom developing equipment

Underwater camera

Concealed umbrella camera

Nikon F SLR camera

Sony digital camera

PHOTOGRAPHY

Written by
ALAN BUCKINGHAM

Studio photography

DK

Daguerreotype in frame

Spy camera concealed in a book

Flash meter

DK

LONDON, NEW YORK, MELBOURNE, MUNICH, AND DELHI

For Cooling Brown Ltd:
Creative director Arthur Brown
Managing editor Amanda Lebentz
Senior designer Tish Jones

For Dorling Kindersley Ltd:
Managing editor Andrew Macintyre
Managing art editor Jane Thomas
Senior editors Fran Jones, Carey Scott
Senior art editor Joanne Connor
Publishing manager Caroline Buckingham
Publishing director Jonathan Metcalf
Picture researcher Sarah Pownall
Production controller Luca Bazzoli
DTP designer Siu Yin Ho
Jacket designer Chris Drew
Special photography Andy Crawford, Dave King
Consultant Chris George
US editor Christine Heilman

This Eyewitness ® Guide has been conceived by
Dorling Kindersley Limited and Editions Gallimard

First American Edition, 2004

Published in the United States by
DK Publishing, Inc., 375 Hudson Street,
New York, New York 10014

04 05 06 07 08 10 9 8 7 6 5 4 3 2 1

Copyright © 2004 Dorling Kindersley Limited

A Cataloging-in-Publication record for this book
is available from the Library of Congress.

ISBN 0-7566-0543-1

Color reproduction by Colourscan, Singapore
Printed in China by Toppan Printing Co., (Shenzhen) Ltd

Discover more at
www.dk.com

Darkroom
enlarger

Polaroid test shots

Victorian photographic plates

Box Brownie

Lightbox and
negatives

Contents

Instant prints

The camera obscura

Long before the invention of photography, people understood the role of light in recording images. When light enters a darkened room through a pinhole in one of the walls, it projects an upside-down image of the world outside onto the opposite wall. Chinese, Greek, and Arabian astronomers have known this for centuries – Aristotle (384–322 BCE) employed the principle to observe solar eclipses. During the Renaissance, Italian artists fitted lenses and mirrors to the pinhole, and the camera obscura (from the Latin for "room" and "dark") was born. Thus, the optics of the camera were in place – but it was centuries before chemists were able to solve the problem of how to permanently record the images.

GETTING THE RIGHT PERSPECTIVE
The Dutch artist Vermeer (1632–75) is renowned for the uncannily accurate perspective, remarkable detail, and realistic natural lighting of his paintings of interiors. There is strong evidence that he created them with the help of images projected by a camera obscura onto the back wall of the room in which he painted.

Upside-down image on screen

Second pinhole faces in opposite direction

Tracing over the projected image

A ROOM WITH TWO VIEWS
This clever contraption, used in Germany in the 1640s, was a portable camera obscura room, shown here with a wall removed. Light entering through pinholes in the outer canvas walls cast images on the transparent paper walls inside. The artist – who climbed inside through a trapdoor in the floor – was able to trace the upside-down images onto the paper.

THE ARTIST'S FRIEND
Table-top camera obscuras, the forerunners of the first photographic cameras, were used as drawing aids by many artists. The devices incorporated lenses with simple sliding mechanisms to allow focusing. They also contained internal mirrors to flip the image the right way up for tracing onto paper.

Hinged lid reveals flat glass viewing screen

Sliding lens to focus image on screen

Table-top camera obscura (c. 1855)

SEASIDE ENTERTAINMENT
Custom-built camera obscuras, such as this one on Margate pier in England, were popular attractions at 19th-century seaside resorts. The building had a revolving mirror and lens on its roof that projected an image onto a circular viewing table in the middle of the darkened room.

SKETCHING ON THE MOVE
Portable camera obscuras were created for artists to use on the road. Often constructed like wigwams or portable tents, they could be set up anywhere for sketching from life. The artist sat inside and traced over the image projected onto a flat desk. This example was made in Paris in the mid-19th century, and is topped by a rotating brass cylinder containing a glass prism and lens.

Adjustable right-angle glass prism and lens capture light and project image downward

The School of Athens, after Raphael by Sir Joshua Reynolds

SECRETIVE USE OF THE CAMERA OBSCURA
Since the early 16th century, artists had been using the camera obscura to project a 3-D view of the world onto flat surfaces for tracing, thus helping them master the difficulties of perspective and proportion. Leonardo da Vinci described his own experiments with the device in his notebooks. Yet more than 200 years later, the method was still a carefully guarded professional secret. Artists did not want it known that they used mechanical aids. English portrait painter Sir Joshua Reynolds (1723–92) owned a camera obscura that could be folded flat and disguised as a book when not in use.

The artist looked through this viewfinder

Leather curtain to keep out light

Drawing surface

Joshua Reynolds' camera obscura (*c.* 1760-80)

19TH-CENTURY CAMERA OBSCURA IN OPERATION
The camera obscura at the Observatory Museum in Grahamstown, South Africa was constructed in the late 1880s by Henry Carter Galpin, an immigrant English jeweler with a passion for optics and astronomy. Set at the top of a four-story tower, it has a rotating prism mechanism in its roof that projects a bird's-eye view of the town onto a polished-metal table. This the only working camera obscura in the southern hemisphere, but there are are several in the northern hemisphere (see pp. 68–69).

The birth of photography

FIRST PHOTOGRAPH
The world's oldest surviving photograph was taken by French inventor Joseph Niépce (1765–1833) in 1826 or 1827. It was produced on a light-sensitive sheet of pewter in an adapted camera obscura. The view is from the upstairs window of Niépce's workroom. The exposure lasted for an incredible eight hours!

IN EARLY-19TH-CENTURY France, a race was on to discover a way of permanently recording images cast by a camera obscura. Two men led the contest: Joseph Niépce and Louis Daguerre. Niépce was the first to produce a lasting photographic image, but it was Daguerre who invented the process that introduced photography to the masses. In 1839, at the French Academy of Science in Paris, he made a grand public announcement of his daguerreotype process. It triggered an explosion of popular interest. Suddenly everyone wanted to be "daguerreotyped." New studios opened all over Paris. The craze for having portraits taken, known as daguerreotypomania, quickly spread through France, across Europe, and to the United States.

EARLY PIONEER
Joseph Niépce began his pioneering research into photographic processes rather late in life, at the age of 51. Ten years later, he produced the world's first permanent photograph. In 1832, at age 67, he went into partnership with Daguerre, but he died just a year later, his work largely unrecognized.

Sliding rear box

Tilting mechanism

THE DAGUERREOTYPE CAMERA
The world's first publicly available daguerreotype camera was made by a Parisian named Alphonse Giroux in 1839. It used the sliding-box principle. Light entered through a lens in the front of one box and fell onto a glass screen at the back of a second box. The rear box was slid back and forth until the image was in focus. To take a picture, the glass screen was replaced with a photographic plate, the lens cover was moved aside, and the exposure was made.

A MIRROR WITH MEMORY
Daguerreotypes were fragile objects. A contemporary newspaper described the silvered metal plate with its often-faint impression as "a mirror with memory." To protect them, the plates were often mounted under glass in ornate frames and cases.

Plate holder

CREATING A PICTURE

Daguerreotype images were made on copper plates coated with silver, carefully cleaned and polished, and treated with iodine and bromine vapors to make them sensitive to light. This process, in which the silver turned to gold-colored silver iodide, was called sensitizing. The unexposed plate was put in the back of the camera, and the exposure made. The plate was then suspended in a special box over mercury vapor to develop the image and make it visible. To stop the silver from continuing to react with light, it was "fixed" with a solution of ordinary salt or hyposulfite of soda.

Double sensitizing box

Polished silver-coated plate

Mercury vapor developing box

Oil lamp for warming mercury

Buffer for polishing plate

Beveler for finishing edges of plate

THE 1840s PHOTOGRAPHER

Daguerreotype equipment was expensive and the process was complex and unreliable. The chemicals could also be dangerous. A photographer in the 1840s was more like a laboratory chemist than an artist.

WHERE ARE ALL THE PEOPLE?

This panoramic daguerreotype of the Seine riverbank in Paris was taken in about 1842 by Charles Chevalier, a photographic equipment maker who worked with both Niépce and Daguerre. The exposure times of 15 minutes or more required by the early cameras meant that pedestrians and carriages simply didn't appear in the picture unless they remained absolutely still.

Image is reversed left-to-right, as all daguerreotypes were

SHOWMAN AND INVENTOR

Louis Daguerre (1787–1851) was a painter, a stage-set designer, and a showman. His Parisian Diorama, a spectacular theatrical light show, was one of the most popular attractions of its day. His desire to create ever more lifelike panoramas and illusions spurred his search for a way of making a permanent photographic record of the images projected by his camera obscura. In other words, he needed a way of fixing images. Finally, in 1839, after many years' work, he announced to the world the discovery of the daguerreotype process.

From negative to positive

WHILE NIÉPCE AND DAGUERRE were at work in France, an English inventor named Henry Fox Talbot was also conducting experiments. His research would result in the invention of the photographic negative. Unlike the daguerreotype, which was a one-time image and could not, therefore, be reproduced, Fox Talbot's calotype negatives could be used to make any number of positive prints. Although revolutionary, his process had drawbacks. Exposure times were long, the method was time-consuming, and the prints were sometimes uneven or faded. A few years later, Frederick Scott Archer's collodion or wet-plate process replaced it and became the predominant form of photography between the 1850s and 1870s.

GHOSTLY SILHOUETTES
Fox Talbot's first photographic experiments in 1834 involved soaking sheets of writing paper in salt and silver nitrate solution, placing objects on them, then exposing them to sunlight. The light-sensitive silver salts darkened where light fell on them, so the objects created a silhouetted image – white on black. Fox Talbot called his pictures photogenic drawings (today we call them photograms).

Calotype photography

The calotype process, first announced by Fox Talbot in 1841, was the culmination of his long struggle to capture the image projected by the camera obscura. The pictures he recorded were made on paper soaked in light-sensitive silver iodide to produce negative images. From these he developed a process for making positive prints on further sheets of paper.

CALOTYPE'S CREATOR
Henry Fox Talbot (1800–77) was a wealthy landowner and an amateur scientist and mathematician. He lived at Lacock Abbey in England, where many of his early photographs were taken. In 1844–46, he published the world's first photographically illustrated book. Called *The Pencil of Nature*, it comprises six bound volumes, each containing four glued-in calotype prints.

Dark tent for preparing wet plates

One of Fox Talbot's earliest negatives, shown actual size

Hand cart

Fox Talbot's handwritten notes

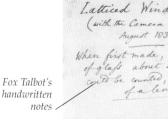

EARLIEST CAMERA NEGATIVE
Fox Talbot experimented with placing light-sensitive sheets of paper in camera obscuras in his attempts to record the images they captured. One of these images is regarded as the world's oldest surviving negative. It shows a lattice window, and was taken with one of his own tiny homemade cameras – nicknamed mousetraps by his wife because they were scattered all around the house.

Calotype positive print

Calotype paper negative

Lightproof box for carrying photographic plates

MAKING A POSITIVE PRINT
Fox Talbot's calotype negatives were made of fine, semi-transparent paper. To make a positive print, he pressed the negative against a sheet of light-sensitive paper and exposed it to sunlight for up to 20 minutes – often in large outdoor printing racks. The print was then fixed with hyposulfite of soda, washed, and dried.

Collodion photography

During the 1840s, all photographs were either daguerreotypes or calotypes – metal plates or flimsy paper negatives. Many attempts had been made to use glass instead, but it proved impossible to get the light-sensitive chemicals to stick to the smooth surface until Archer's collodion method solved the problem. His so-called wet plates were more sensitive to light than calotypes (so camera exposures could be shorter), and the quality of the image was sharper and more detailed.

INVENTOR OF COLLODION
In 1851, Frederick Scott Archer, an English sculptor and photographer, published details of a successful method of making light-sensitive glass plates. His collodion process revolutionized photography – within five years, it had virtually replaced daguerreotypes and calotypes throughout the world.

Wet-plate negative

WET-PLATE CASE
Freshly prepared wet plates had to be carried quickly in a lightproof box from darkroom to camera before they dried out, then back again for developing once a picture had been taken.

Toner   Varnish   Fixer

WET-PLATE CHEMICALS
Collodion – nitrated cotton dissolved in alcohol and ether – hardens on exposure to air. In Archer's process, glass plates were coated with collodion and potassium iodide, dipped in silver nitrate to make them light-sensitive, then exposed in the camera while still wet. The image was immediately developed, fixed, and washed, and later varnished.

Mahogany sliding box camera

THE PORTABLE DARKROOM
Using lightproof tents that folded out of travel boxes or handcarts, photographers were able to work on location. Taking pictures outdoors, however, was difficult and dangerous. Preparing the plates had to be done swiftly, in complete darkness, and with enough water available to keep them wet. The air beneath the canvas sheet would have been full of toxic fumes.

Chest of chemicals for sensitizing and developing plates

DOCUMENTING WAR
The Crimean War (1853–56) was the first military conflict ever to be photographed. English photographer Roger Fenton recorded images of the front line before and after battles, and took formally posed shots of groups of soldiers in camp, such as this one in 1855. Lengthy exposure times meant action pictures were impossible.

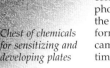

The Victorian studio

WITH THE INVENTION of the daguerreotype, photography studios, known as parlors, began to spring up everywhere. For the first time, ordinary people could have their likeness taken, and everyone wanted to be photographed. Sitting for a portrait in one of the first studios was hot and uncomfortable. Subjects were often clamped into chairs and asked to sit motionless under glass in full sunlight. The process became less grueling with the development of more light-sensitive photographic plates and the use of magnesium flash and electric lighting, which shortened exposure times. Elaborate props and backgrounds were used, and poses became more natural. Meanwhile, a whole industry was born, mass-producing photographic cards and prints, and manufacturing albums, frames, and cases. It was boom time for almost anyone who wanted to set up as a professional photographer.

THROWING LIGHT ON A SUBJECT
Because bright daylight was needed to make an exposure, early studios were usually built of glass – like greenhouses. In towns, they were often on the roof of the photographer's building. This is the studio and printing works Fox Talbot established in Reading, England. Here, he was able to set up a studio portrait, take the photograph, and make contact prints from his calotype negative, all in one place.

ORNAMENTAL KEEPSAKES
Victorian portraits were often inset into jewelry – brooches, pendants, lockets, and even cufflinks and signet rings. Daguerreotypes and collodion prints swiftly displaced miniature portrait paintings. In fact, many painters of miniatures, seeing their livelihoods disappearing, reinvented themselves as studio photographers.

SCENE OF PROSPERITY
Having your photograph taken was much like sitting for a portrait painter, although it didn't take as long, of course, and it was a lot cheaper. People used photographs to impress others with their social standing and so most were looking for a similar result – a dignified, fairly formal pose, with standard props chosen to suggest a wealthy lifestyle. It was no surprise, then, that early photographers tended to imitate artists and create pictures that looked like paintings.

Victorian plate camera with bellows

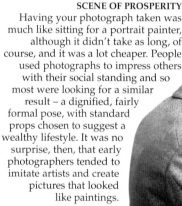

Movable plate

Back

Front

CALLING-CARD CAMERA
This plate camera, made in the 1860s by John Henry Dallmeyer, a German living in London, was an early form of the passport camera. It was designed for taking calling-card or *cartes-de-visite* portraits. After one shot, the plate was moved to a new position and another exposure was made, until the plate contained four standard-sized 3 x 4 in (7.5 x 10 cm) pictures. Other, similar cameras equipped with four separate lenses were able to take four portraits with one exposure.

CELEBRITY PORTRAITS

In the 1860s, collecting photographic prints of well-known people was so popular that the craze was termed "cardomania" by the press. Remember that printed photographs in newspapers and magazines were still unknown. Until the emergence of these cards, paintings and reproductions of engravings were the only images most ordinary people had ever seen.

English scientist Michael Faraday (c. 1860)

Napoleon III and Empress Eugénie (c. 1865)

FAMILY HEIRLOOMS

Collections of photographs were shown off in family albums, which were handed down from generation to generation. They took both the standard-sized *cartes-de-visite* and the slightly larger cabinet prints. Pictures of family and friends were mounted alongside portraits of famous people, and album pages were often decorated with images of contemporary scenes. This one, which dates from about 1870, shows the Crimean War.

Neck support

Magnesium powder

EXPLODING FLASH

In the 1880s, the first indoor studio lights used magnesium, which burns with an intense white light. Photographers would ignite a small alcohol burner and then blow magnesium powder into the flame at exactly the moment when the photograph was taken. The result was a brilliant flash – unfortunately followed by smoke, smell, and a fine covering of white ash.

Painted backdrop of conventional country landscape

Adjustable brace

Studio props suggest a comfortable interior

Back support

Victorian clamp

STAYING PERFECTLY STILL

In the early days of studio photography, camera exposure times were very long – anywhere between 10 seconds and a minute. Sitters had to remain completely motionless while the shutter was open or their portrait would be blurred. Special clamps were often used to support the head and back and to ensure that there was no twitching or fidgeting. Smiling was frowned on, and blinking was forbidden. This probably explains why many portraits of the time look so tense and unnatural.

Movement and color

IN 1871, A NEW KIND OF photographic plate was introduced that transformed photography. The gelatin dry plate was invented by Richard Maddox. It was much easier to use than the existing collodion wet plate, but perhaps more importantly, it was far more sensitive to light. This meant that exposure times were shorter, cameras could be hand-held instead of requiring tripods, and for the first time successful photographs could be taken of moving subjects. Less successful was the ongoing search for a way of producing color pictures. Progress was slow. Successful experiments were taking place with three-color lantern projectors. It was not until 1907, however, when the Lumière brothers produced the first Autochromes, that a process for creating color transparencies became readily available. Unfortunately, color prints were still decades away.

DOCTOR'S DISCOVERY
Richard Maddox was an English doctor and amateur photographer. Finding that the ether fumes given off by collodion (see p. 11) affected his health, he set out to invent an alternative. In 1871, he announced the success of experiments in which he coated glass plates with an emulsion of silver bromide in gelatin. Unlike collodion, the plates remained light-sensitive even when dry.

Half-silvered mirror

Front cover removed to reveal lens and shutter mechanism

Viewfinder

CANDID CAMERA
The Fallowfield Facile camera of about 1890 was basically a large box with a small hole in the front for the lens. Inside were 12 glass plates that dropped from one compartment to another after each one had been exposed and before the camera needed reloading. The Facile and its like were known as "detective" cameras because they were considered relatively unobtrusive for their time. Carried under the arm disguised in brown paper, they could be used to take the kind of candid shots that would have been impossible before.

Opening for lens

Negative photographe with green camera filter

STREET LIFE
The increased light-sensitivity of dry plates – coupled with improvements in lens design – meant much shorter exposures than in the past. For the first time, pictures could be taken at shutter speeds of fractions of a second rather than several seconds or even minutes. Instead of awkwardly posed portraits and unpopulated landscapes, it was now possible to take much more spontaneous photographs in which people moved naturally, without having to stand still for the camera. The term "snapshot" was born.

Rush hour in Piccadilly, London

AIM AND SHOOT
By the 1890s, cameras for the amateur were becoming steadily smaller. The first practical hand-held models often had no viewfinders, so photographers took aim by centering their subject in the middle of a "V" shape on the top of the camera before firing the shutter.

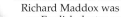

PROJECTING COLOR IMAGES

Photographers had long known that any color can be created by mixing red, green, and blue light in the correct proportions. It was the principle behind Maxwell's experiments (see right). In the US, a printer and photographer named Frederic Eugene Ives created a whole range of "Kromskop" cameras, table-top viewers, and projectors that could produce color images using red, green, and blue filters.

Kromskop table-top viewer, 1895

Colored lens filter

Triple-lens projector

Red was the most difficult color to reproduce

FIRST COLOR PHOTOGRAPH

In 1861, a Scottish professor of physics named James Clerk Maxwell demonstrated what is often claimed to be the first color photograph. It was an image of a plaid bow, produced from three black-and-white negatives that were photographed and projected with red, green, and blue filters. At the time, plates were not sensitive to red light, so it was lucky that the experiment worked at all.

LEADING LIGHTS

The first practical method for creating color transparencies was launched in 1907 by French brothers Auguste and Louis Lumière. They took their inspiration from the Impressionist painter Seurat's "pointilliste" technique of tricking the eye into seeing colors built up from tiny dots of paint. Their Autochrome plates had a coating of minute grains of starch dyed red, green, and blue. The grains acted as filters on top of a positive black-and-white image to produce an optical effect of full color.

Negative photographed with blue camera filter

Negative photographed with red camera filter

The Lumière brothers

Blue projection filter

Red projection filter

Green projection filter

Adjustable focusing rail

THREE-COLOR PROJECTION

This projection apparatus from about 1900 is very similar to the ones used in Ives's triple-color "Kromskop" system. Using a special camera fitted with a system of mirrors or prisms and red, green, and blue filters, three different black-and-white negatives of the same scene were produced. The negatives were then placed in the apparatus and projected using matching colored filters. When the three projected images were superimposed on one another, they produced a full-color picture.

COLOR AUTOCHROMES

Autochrome transparencies were very popular until the 1930s. It has been estimated that around 20 million were taken, and leading photographers of the day all tried them out. The subtlety of the color was a revelation, but exposure times were long. Like this shot, the best photographs were taken outdoors in sunshine.

Photography – the new art

IMITATING CLASSICAL ART
Early photographs – especially portraits – were posed and formal, like paintings. Compositions were influenced by Renaissance and Pre-Raphaelite styles, and pictures often had religious or allegorical themes. For these reasons, the style was known as High Art photography. In pictures such as *The Passing of Arthur* (1890), Julia Margaret Cameron used actors in costume.

When photography emerged in the middle of the 19th century, many painters greeted it with horror, thinking it would rob them of their livelihood. "From today, painting is dead!" responded the artist Paul Delaroche on being shown a daguerreotype for the first time. Some artists dismissed photography in public but in private used it to help them produce more accurate drawings and paintings (as they had always done with the camera obscura). Others welcomed it, even if they were unsure whether it was an art or a science. In the years that followed, photographers explored the artistic possibilities of the new medium, initially making pictures that were much like paintings, but ultimately producing photographs that were an art form in their own right.

The Gleaners (1857) by Millet

BACK TO NATURE
A backlash against High Art came in the form of a new style known as "pictorialism" or "naturalistic" photography, spearheaded in England by P. H. Emerson. He rejected artificial subjects in favor of natural scenes that used composition and light to evoke mood. His pictures were sometimes like paintings, too – but of a different kind. They borrowed from the work of artists such as Jean-Francois Millet, Jean-Baptiste-Camille Corot, and the Impressionists, and used soft-focus effects, textured papers, and hand tinting.

Ricking the Reed (1886)
by P. H. Emersen

Background shot in Robinson's own yard

COMPOSITE PICTURES
Henry Peach Robinson was a leading figure in the High Art movement. His famous photograph of *The Lady of Shalott* (1861) borrows from both Tennyson's poem and Millais' painting of Ophelia from *Hamlet*. Many of his photographs were multiple prints. He would first sketch the picture he wanted to make – just like a painter – then separately photograph the individual components. Finally he would combine the cut-out figures, masks, and backgrounds and make one large contact print.

Ophelia (1852) by John Millais

Familiar objects take on an abstract quality

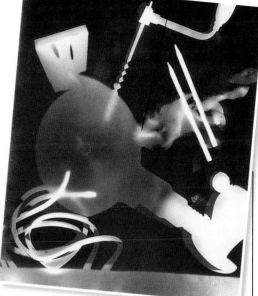

Solarization partially fogs the print

A NEW LIGHT ON EVERYDAY LIFE
Early in the 20th century, photographers such as Paul Strand and Edward Weston began to take a new kind of photograph. Pictures such as Strand's *Ceramic and Fruit* (1916) illustrate how they deliberately chose everyday subjects that would previously have been dismissed as too ordinary to photograph. Strand shot simple still-life arrangements in natural light, avoided any darkroom trickery, and revealed a richness of form, texture, and pattern that becomes almost abstract.

EARLY ABSTRACT PHOTOGRAPHS
American artist Man Ray was one of the first to produce abstract photographs. In 1920 he began making photograms – or "Rayographs" as he called them – by arranging objects on a sheet of photographic paper, exposing it to light, and then developing the paper to create a silhouette-like print. Sometimes he "solarized" the picture by briefly turning on the light while it was developing.

The Cotton Exchange (1873) by Edgar Degas

PHOTOGRAPHY INFLUENCES PAINTING
French painter Edgar Degas was an early fan of photography. Many of his paintings of horses and horse races owe much to the photo-sequences of Eadweard Muybridge (see p. 34). Paintings such as this public scene were composed in the style of photographs. People were cropped abruptly, and painted in poses that only a camera would have captured. Perspective was sometimes exaggerated.

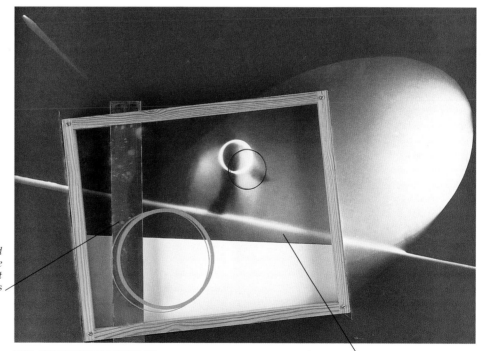

Metal rule and wooden frame create abstract shapes

Main subject photographed in Robinson's studio

Photogram forms background to work

THE ART OF PHOTOMONTAGE
Like Man Ray, Hungarian photographer László Moholy-Nagy was influenced by modern art movements such as Cubism and Dadaism. In the 1920s, he taught at the Bauhaus school of art and design in Germany, where he encouraged experimentation – the combination of photography with painting and drawing, photograms, solarization, multiple exposures, montage, and darkroom manipulation. This work, *Composition* (1926), is a collage of real objects and painted circles on a background photogram produced using carefully controlled lighting.

Photography for everyone

THE STORY OF POPULAR photography is largely the story of one man, George Eastman, and the company he founded, Kodak. He not only produced the first reliable point-and-shoot cameras, he also devised a system that meant ordinary people no longer had to worry about developing and printing the film. When you finished your roll of film, you simply mailed your camera to Kodak. Back came your pictures, along with the camera reloaded with new film. Eastman's marketing slogan was "You press the button, we do the rest." All subsequent innovations in popular photography, from Brownies and Instamatics, through color film, to autofocus and motorized and digital cameras, have concentrated on achieving the same ease of use.

AFFORDABLE PHOTOGRAPHY
Kodak's Baby Brownie of 1934 was made of plastic, so was perfect for inexpensive mass-production. The camera took standard 127 roll film which produced tiny black-and-white "vest-pocket" photos only 2.5 x 1.6 in (64 x 40 mm) in size. This advertisement features one of the famous "Kodak Girls," shown against the distinctive yellow and red Kodak background.

INSIDE THE FIRST KODAK CAMERA
At the front of the Kodak No. 1, introduced in 1888, was a cylindrical shutter inside which was a lens. There was no focusing and no viewfinder. You simply pointed the camera at your subject, pulled a string to set the shutter, and pressed the button to make an exposure. Then you advanced the roll of film in the back of the camera for the next shot. A round screen masked light that came through the lens and fell onto the film, so early Box Brownie photographs were circular. After taking 100 pictures, you sent the camera to Kodak for processing.

Circular picture mask

Key to advance film

20-ft (6-m) roll of film

String-pull to set shutter

MAN WITH A MISSION
Born in 1854 in New York State, George Eastman left school at 14 to work in insurance and banking. At 24, he bought his first photographic outfit – an expensive and cumbersome "packhorse load" made up of camera, tripod, canvas darkroom, tanks, boxes, and chemicals. He decided to simplify the whole process and "make the camera as convenient as the pencil." In 1888 he registered the name Kodak and started the company that pioneered cheap and easy-to-use photography.

Monkeying around for the camera (c. 1959)

THE CAMERA ANY CHILD COULD USE
George Eastman's dream was to create an inexpensive camera so easy to operate that even a child could use it. He achieved this in 1900 with the launch of the Box Brownie. To reinforce the message, the packaging featured pixie-like Brownies created by Canadian illustrator Palmer Cox. The Box Brownie cost $1 in the US.

CHANGING FILM FORMATS

Since the 1930s, 35 mm has been the standard film format, but there have been many attempts over the years to introduce easier-to-load alternatives. Instamatic cameras, using cartridge film that could be simply slotted into the back of the camera, were a Kodak invention, with 50 million sold between 1963 and 1970. In 1972, Kodak shrank it to the tinier 110 Pocket Instamatic. In 1983, the Disc camera was launched, but it never caught on with the public and became extinct within four years. In 1996, there followed a new compact film format in a drop-in cassette, Advanced Photo System (APS).

126 Instamatic

COLORFUL VACATION MEMORIES

Although Kodacolor and Agfacolor negative film was launched in the early 1940s, it was not until the 1970s that color prints became widespread. Before then almost all family photos were in black-and-white, unless they were slides. Now it is difficult to imagine a time when vacation snapshots were not bright, sunny, and full of color.

110 Pocket
Instamatic

Cartridge film

*Agfacolor 35-mm
transparency film*

*35-mm color
slides in
cardboard
mounts*

*Kodachrome film
for making slides*

ERA OF THE SLIDESHOW

The first commonly used color film produced transparencies, not negatives. It was difficult to make prints from them, so photos were displayed by projecting the slides onto a wall screen, or they were looked at with a special slide viewer – hence the term "slideshow." Both Kodak's Kodachrome and its rival Agfacolor (1936) used a film base coated with very thin layers of film emulsion sensitive to red, green, and blue light.

*Camera in
printer dock*

School camera-club outing

PHOTOGRAPHY BECOMES A FAVORITE HOBBY

By the end of World War II, cheap cameras were everywhere. They were easy to use, and they took reasonable pictures. Film costs were lower, too. All this made photography accessible to everyone. Many children growing up in the 1950s and '60s joined camera clubs at school, and at home they developed film and made prints in temporary darkrooms set up above the kitchen sink, over the bathtub, or in the garage. Their pictures were mostly black-and-white. Color processing and printing at home was too expensive and too difficult for all but the most dedicated hobbyists.

QUICK AND EASY COLOR PRINTS

Digital cameras have made the photo-processing laboratory obsolete. There is no film, so no developing, either. Color prints can easily be made on an inkjet printer linked to a computer. Alternatively, prints can be produced by placing the camera in a special printer dock (as here) and downloading image files direct from the memory card.

Classic camera designs

THE DRIVING FORCE BEHIND camera design at the beginning of the 20th century was the invention of roll film. First introduced in 1889 by pioneer George Eastman, roll film meant that cameras could be much smaller than those that still used bulky photographic plates. But in the years that followed, there was a bewildering variety of film formats. It took some time before the industry standardized on medium-format 120 roll film and small-format 35-mm cassettes. Cameras, too, came in many shapes and sizes – and with increasingly sophisticated features. From a design point of view, the major issue was how the picture was previewed – through a separate viewfinder, through a second viewing lens (twin-lens reflex), or through the picture-taking lens itself (single-lens reflex).

THE VIEW THROUGH THE LENS
Most early plate or "view" cameras did not have viewfinders. The shot was framed and focused by looking at an upside-down image on a glass screen at the back of the camera. Once the photographer was satisfied, the shutter was closed and the photographic plate or film was loaded.

Viewfinder

Lens and shutter unit

Front of camera moves back and forth on baseboard to focus

FOLDING ROLL FILM CAMERAS
Compact folding cameras that could be loaded in daylight with roll film cartridges were pioneered by Kodak at the end of the 19th century. They were to prove popular for many years to come. More than 300,000 Kodak No. 3A Autographic cameras were produced between 1914 and 1934. Although described as a pocket camera, at just over 10 in (25 cm) in height, it was rather large.

Viewfinder mounted on lens

Folding lens and bellows unit

Rangefinder (focusing device)

Flashgun triggers shutter to open when it is fired

LARGE-FORMAT PLATE CAMERAS
Today, wood has been replaced by metal and the baseboard by a monorail, but otherwise the large-format plate camera is little changed since the mid-19th century. The bellows design is still useful for architectural, still-life, and studio work. Large sheets of film produce big negatives or transparencies that give very high-quality images. This 1930 Gandolfi camera was used for taking mug shots of offenders in British prisons.

THE FASCINATION WITH PHOTOGRAPHY
The popularity of illustrated magazines in the 1940s and '50s stimulated public interest in photography and provoked a constant thirst for photographs, particularly of celebrities. In 1947, *Picture Post*, one of the most successful magazines, devoted a front cover not just to an aspiring movie actress but also to the two photographers commissioned to take her picture.

LEGENDARY ENGINEERING

The Leica was designed between 1911 and 1913 by Oscar Barnack, an employee of the German firm Leitz, which manufactured optical instruments. Barnack wanted a compact camera he could take on mountaineering trips, so he used offcuts of the 35-mm film available from movie studios, which gave smaller negatives than most other cameras of the time. From the start, Leica cameras benefited from the company's experience of making top-quality lenses.

Shutter speed dial

Viewfinder

High-quality lens

LAUNCHING THE LEICA

At its launch at the Leipzig Spring Fair in 1925, the Leica was described as a miniature camera. Despite initial doubts, the pictures from its 35-mm negatives proved excellent, and in the 1930s it became the camera of choice for photographers such as Henri Cartier-Bresson.

THE AMERICAN PRESS PHOTOGRAPHER'S CAMERA

The Speed Graphic was the camera used by the vast majority of American press photographers over a period of more than half a century. First introduced in 1912, it used 4-x-5-in plates that could be developed in time to meet newspaper deadlines. Later models were fitted with accessories such as large wire-frame viewfinders and flashguns, but the basic design remained unchanged until the 1950s – when this picture of a group of photographers jostling for position was taken.

Wire-frame viewfinder

The arrival of reflex cameras

Reflex cameras use a mirror system to project an image of what the camera sees onto a glass viewing screen so that you can frame and focus the picture exactly as you wish. Single-lens reflex (SLR) cameras allow you to look through the camera lens itself, so that you can see what will be recorded on the film or image sensor. In principle, SLR cameras work in a way similar to the reflex camera obscura (see p. 6). By contrast, twin-lens reflex (TLR) cameras show the view through a secondary lens situated just above the camera lens.

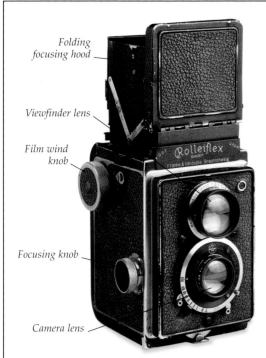

Folding focusing hood

Viewfinder lens

Film wind knob

Focusing knob

Camera lens

CANDID CAMERA?
A photographer associated with the Rolleiflex is Robert Doisneau. The camera was unobtrusive and quiet – ideal for his spontaneous shots of Parisian street life. Nevertheless, after a notorious court case, he was forced to admit that his most famous picture, "The Kiss" (1950), had been staged.

TWIN-LENS REFLEX CAMERAS
Cameras with two lenses – one to look through and one to take the picture – date from the 1880s, but they used plates and were bulky and unpopular. The 1928 German Rolleiflex ("roll film reflex") changed all that. It was the first successful medium-format roll film TLR camera. It took 2¼-in-square (6-x-6-cm) film that could be contact-printed or enlarged, and it was made of metal and precision-engineered.

A Rolleiflex held at waist level

USING A TWIN-LENS REFLEX
A focusing hood on top of the camera flipped up to reveal a ground glass screen. A magnified image of the scene was projected onto the screen through the viewfinder lens. Rotating the focusing knob moved both lenses closer to or farther from the film.

PROFESSIONAL 35-MM PHOTOGRAPHY
By the 1960s, newspapers and magazines were accepting 35-mm negatives and transparencies for reproduction. Photographers were also adopting the new complete systems of interchangeable lenses and accessories. Nikon equipment, in particular, was compact and rugged enough for the sort of assignment to northwest Canada where Paul Almasy shot this picture of a native Inuit woman.

Ihagee Exakta (1937)

Pentaprism viewfinder

Zeiss Contax S (1949)

Nikon F (1959)

SINGLE-LENS REFLEX CAMERAS
The first 35-mm SLR camera was the German Kine Exakta in 1936. A hinged mirror inside the camera projected a reversed image onto a glass viewing screen and lifted out of the way of the film when the picture was taken. In 1949, Zeiss's Contax S introduced a pentaprism and mirror system – still used today – that reversed and flipped the image so that it appeared correctly in the viewfinder. The Nikon F, launched in 1959, was the Japanese firm's first SLR.

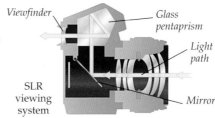

Viewfinder

Glass pentaprism

Light path

SLR viewing system

Mirror

EQUIPPED FOR ANY EVENTUALITY
Illustrating the point that a professional photographer should always be prepared for any photo opportunity, Hungarian-born Paul Almasy (1906–2003) is equipped with a Nikon F 35-mm SLR, a Rolleiflex TLR, and a medium-format Hasselblad. Almasy claimed to have visited every country in the world but two during his career as a leading photojournalist.

ALL THE RAGE IN THE 1960S

In London in the Swinging Sixties, fashion and pop photographers such as Patrick Lichfield (left) and David Bailey became as famous as the celebrities they photographed. The Hasselblad was their trademark camera. It was light, simple to use, and could just as easily be hand-held or tripod mounted. It had interchangeable lenses and interchangeable film backs. And its 2¼-in-square (6-x-6-cm) transparencies produced the sort of high-quality results that the glossy magazines demanded.

Hasselblad on a tripod

Pop-up magnifier for focusing on detail

THE VERSATILE HASSELBLAD

The first of the legendary Swedish Hasselblads appeared in 1948. It was a medium-format SLR camera designed for professional photographers. One of the keys to its success was that the 120 roll film it used was loaded into a detachable device fitted to the back of the camera. This meant that photographers could quickly switch backs containing films of different speeds and types during the same photo session.

Nikon F

Focusing screen

Light path through lens

Rolleiflex twin-lens reflex

Hasselblad with telephoto lens

MODERN STUDIO PHOTOGRAPHY

The Hasselblad's 120 roll film transparencies or negatives are more than three times the size of 35-mm ones. This results in higher quality when images are enlarged. Through-the-lens framing is also extremely accurate. These features are especially important for studio work, such as food or advertising photography, when the aim is to capture clarity of detail, such as the droplets of moisture on these rose petals.

Anatomy of a 35-mm SLR camera

35-MM FILM
Film strips come in light-proof metal cassettes. After each exposure, the film is wound out of the cassette onto a spool in the camera. When finished, the film is wound back into the cassette for processing.

For many years, the 35-mm single-lens reflex (SLR) has been the most popular camera for serious amateur photographers. It has been widely used by professionals, too, especially on location. In relation to its size, 35-mm film produces good image quality. The SLR design also has many advantages – one is that you can see through the lens itself when you look through the viewfinder, so you can preview exactly how your picture will be framed. Early 35-mm SLRs were mostly manual. You had to set the shutter speed and aperture yourself, and focus the lens. Over the years, many sophisticated features have been added, such as automatic focusing and exposure metering, zoom lenses, built-in flash, motor-drive film mechanisms, and liquid-crystal (LCD) screens for data display.

Shutter release

Shutter speed dial

Film rewind/back cover release knob

Exposure counter

Lens lock release lever

Front view of camera

HOW A CLASSIC 35-MM SLR CAMERA WORKS
Light enters the camera through the lens (see artwork opposite). Initially it is directed up into the viewfinder where the picture can be previewed. When the shutter release is pressed, the shutter opens briefly and a mirror flips quickly out of the way so that light is focused onto the film and an exposure is made. The shutter speed controls the length of time that the film is exposed to light, and the aperture setting alters the diameter of an opening inside the lens, so controlling how much light falls on the film.

Body covering

Lens mount

Front board assembly

Pentaprism retainer plate

Viewfinder eyepiece

Pentaprism retainer spring

Pentaprism

Main body

Viewfinder eyepiece

Shutter curtain

Film take-up spool

Film pressure plate

Back cover

Rear view with cover open

Tripod socket hole

Hole for film rewind button

Battery chamber

Bottom cover assembly

Cover frame

Nameplate ring

Front lens frame retainer plate

Front lens group

Installing ring retainer plate

Supporter ring retainer plate

Supporter ring

Lens barrel assembly

Grip sensors shut down LCD displays to conserve power when camera is not being held

Pop-up flash unit

Viewfinder

Light from subject

Light split by mirror

Sensor analyzes image contrast

Light entering a camera

HOW AUTOFOCUS WORKS

Some of the light entering the lens is diverted away from the viewfinder and onto a sensor similar to those used in digital cameras. The sensor analyzes the image by looking for the area of greatest contrast, on the basis that dark tones with hard edges are more likely to be in focus than gray tones with soft edges. This data is used to adjust the focus of the lens.

Sensors read metal strips on the film cassette to detect which type of film is being used

Autofocus zoom lens

Light enters camera

Motor drives advance film and reset shutter after each shot

ADVANCED AUTOFOCUS CAMERAS

Modern high-quality SLR cameras are packed with electronics. In fact, their automated systems are so sophisticated that they can be used pretty much as point-and-shoot models. However, they also offer manual option (known as override). This means that in certain situations the photographer can choose to take control of focusing, set the lens aperture, or select a shutter speed – instead of leaving it all to the camera's built-in sensors and microprocessors.

DATA DISPLAY

LCD screens show exactly what the camera is doing. When set to aperture priority (A), you choose the aperture and the camera calculates the correct shutter speed. When set to shutter priority (S), you choose the shutter speed, and the camera works out the right aperture.

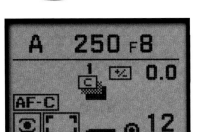

A   250 F8
1
c   ± 0.0
AF-C
□ [ ] ■ □ 12

Speed dial knob

Film speed indicator

Shutter speed dial

Shutter release

Top cover

Hot shoe

Rewind shaft

Film rewind/ back cover release knob

Film rewind crank

Cover frame

Counter dial cover

Exposure counter dial

Counter dial housing

Wind lever install spring

Film wind lever

Wind lever collar

Top cover assembly

Aperture ring

Focusing ring

Opening and closing plate

Rear lens group

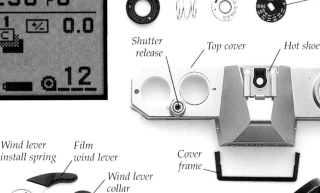

Diaphragm blade

Installing ring

Main barrel assembly

Top view

Camera lenses

A CAMERA LENS IS ACTUALLY a series of lenses through which light passes when it enters the camera. The lens acts as the eye of the camera. First, it ensures that as much of what it sees as possible is precisely focused on the film or digital sensor so that the photograph is sharp, not blurred. Second, it controls how much light is let into the camera so the photo is correctly exposed. It does this by means of a variable "aperture," a hole in the center of the lens that can be opened to admit more light or closed to admit less light. Third, the type of lens determines how much of the scene it sees is recorded. A wide-angle lens sees and records a lot. A telephoto lens sees less, but magnifies what it does see, like a telescope. The lens's angle of view is known as its "focal length."

THREE TIMES MORE RANGE
Before zoom lenses were invented, the designer of this Italian Rectaflex Rotor camera of about 1952 came up with an ingenious idea to give photographers more flexibility. Three lenses of differing focal lengths were fitted to a revolving plate at the front of a 35-mm SLR camera so that the photographer could switch from one to another almost instantly.

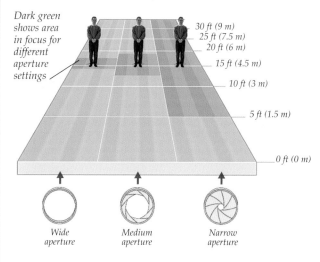

Dark green shows area in focus for different aperture settings

30 ft (9 m)
25 ft (7.5 m)
20 ft (6 m)
15 ft (4.5 m)
10 ft (3 m)
5 ft (1.5 m)
0 ft (0 m)

Wide aperture   *Medium aperture*   *Narrow aperture*

VARYING DEPTH OF FIELD
Lenses struggle to get everything in a photograph in focus. When objects close to the camera are sharp, then those far away are likely to be blurred – and vice versa. "Depth of field" is the term used to define how much of the scene will be in sharp focus. This is affected by the lens aperture. A wide aperture gives a shallow depth of field, which means that focusing has to be very specific. With a narrow aperture, most elements in the shot should be in focus.

Wide-angle lens

THE WIDER ANGLE
As its name suggests, a wide-angle lens has a wide angle of view. It takes in two or three times as much as we can see without moving our eyes from side to side. A wide-angle lens was used to take this shot of a team of huskies. The lenses are also often used for taking photos indoors where space is tight, or to create panoramic landscape shots.

Telephoto lens

Monopods steady bulky fast telephoto lenses

IN ON THE ACTION
Sports photographers often use long, or ultra, telephoto lenses. They want their pictures to look as if they have been shot as close to the action as possible, so when we look at them we feel we are right in the thick of the event. They also need fast shutter speeds to freeze movement. The so-called "fast" wide-aperture lenses that satisfy such requirements are large and expensive.

Polarizing filter

Yellow filter

Red filter

Shot with starburst filter

CREATING SPECIAL EFFECTS
A filter is an attachment, usually made of glass or plastic, that is placed over a lens to alter the way in which light enters the camera. Filters can change an image in a wide variety of ways. Color filters, for example, are often used in black-and-white photography to darken or lighten gray tones. Polarizing filters reduce reflections and boost the blue of skies. There are also special effects filters – one, called a starburst, turns bright lights into pointed stars.

Iris diaphragm controls lens aperture

ANATOMY OF A LENS
A camera lens contains lots of lenses, or lens elements, usually arranged in groups. The groups can be moved back and forth to bring the image in and out of focus and, in zoom lenses, to vary the focal length. This classic lens has two lens groups. The diaphragm blades between them open and close the aperture. Changing aperture and focus is done manually by turning rings on the barrel of the lens. Modern motorized cameras can do this automatically.

Lens group

Diaphragm blades open and close lens aperture

Lens group

Aperture ring

Focus ring

EYE OF THE LENS
The hole in a camera lens is called the aperture. It is constructed from a series of overlapping blades that can vary the diameter of the opening. The system of "f numbers" (or "f-stops") indicates the size of the aperture. When wide open, a lot of light enters the camera, so a shorter exposure (shutter speed) is needed. When narrowed, less light enters, so a longer exposure is required. The "speed" of the lens is its maximum aperture – a fast f/1.8 lens lets in four times as much light as a slower f/3.5 lens.

CLOSE CALL
A telephoto lens is like a telescope – it magnifies the image so that objects appear larger. This makes it perfect for photojournalists and sports and wildlife photographers, who cannot get close to their subjects. The large telephoto lens shown here is a "fast" lens. It has a very wide maximum aperture, so it can capture a lot of light, making possible the fast shutter speeds needed for action photography.

ALL-AROUND VIEW
An extreme wide-angle lens is called a "fisheye" lens. It usually has an angle of view of 180 degrees and produces characteristically curved horizontals and verticals. This shot was taken with a circular fisheye lens from the top of the Great Pyramid of Cheops in Egypt.

Circular fisheye lens

In the darkroom

WITH DIGITAL CAMERAS THAT do not use any film and inkjet printers that can print out photographs in seconds, it's hardly surprising that the home darkroom is not so commonly used as it once was. However, many photographers still enjoy the greater creativity offered by the conventional process of developing film, putting negatives into an enlarger to magnify the image, exposing the light-sensitive photographic paper, then developing, fixing, and washing the print before hanging it up to dry. It is still the best way to understand how film photography works. Black-and-white processing is illustrated here because, although color developing and printing can also be done in a home darkroom, it is more difficult to achieve successful results.

Thermometer

Chemical measuring jar

Lightproof developing tank

DEVELOPING FILM
To process a roll of 35-mm film, it must be removed from its cassette, wound onto a spiral, and then inserted into a lightproof developing tank – a tricky procedure in the dark. Once the film is in the tank, however, developing can be done with the light on. Developer, stop bath, and fixing solutions are diluted and kept at the correct working temperature before being added to the developing tank in sequence. Then the film is washed and dried.

Developed film on a spiral

Squeegee tongs to remove excess water after washing

Red filter allows "safe" light to be used before exposure

Framing bars for neat edges to print

Timer for setting length of exposure

Photographic paper

Negatives

Glass cover

Scissors for cutting paper and negatives

Magnifier for checking focus of print before exposing paper

Negative carrier

USING AN ENLARGER
Before a negative can be turned into a print, it needs to be enlarged and exposed onto light-sensitive photographic paper. The negative is inserted into the enlarger in a special negative carrier. The head of the enlarger is raised to make the image bigger or lowered to make it smaller, and the lens is focused so that the image is sharp. Finally, a sheet of paper is positioned on the baseboard, the red filter is removed, and it is exposed for a calculated length of time.

MAKING A CONTACT SHEET
Photographers often make a single print of all the negatives on a roll of film. This makes it easier to decide which are worth enlarging. The negative strips are laid out on a sheet of paper – with a piece of glass on top to keep them flat – and briefly exposed to light while in contact with the paper – hence the term contact sheet. The sheet and negative strips, stored in protective sleeves, can be kept together for future reference.

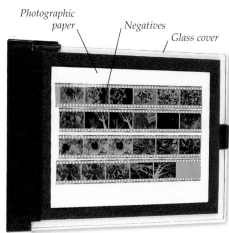

40 sec

20 sec

10 sec

5 sec

TESTING EXPOSURES
Estimating how long the paper should be exposed for requires a certain amount of guesswork, based on experience. Often, photographers make a test strip to see the effect of different exposure times. A sheet of paper is placed under the enlarger and, masking a section at a time, it is then exposed to light one strip after another for set periods of time.

Print hanging up to dry

Red safelight

Making prints

Photographic paper is coated with a light-sensitive layer of silver halide emulsion – much like film. When exposed under the lens of an enlarger, it reacts to the light passing through the negative and forms a latent image – a positive version of the photographic negative. This image is revealed by soaking the print in a developing solution that makes the picture visible.

Image starts to appear

Plastic tray

Tongs

Final image is fixed

Stop bath halts development

1 DEVELOPING THE PRINT
Working in a darkroom lit only by a red safelight, the exposed photographic paper is put into a tray containing the developer, a chemical solution that reacts to the exposed silver halides and turns them into the black metallic silver that forms the image.

2 STOPPING THE PROCESS
When the print has developed to give a good, clear image, it is transferred to a second tray containing the stop bath. This solution, which is usually a weak acid, neutralizes the developer and stops the process.

3 FIXING THE IMAGE
The third tray contains a fixing solution. This turns any unexposed silver halides into soluble salts that can be washed away under running water. Once the paper has been washed, the light can be switched on – the image will be permanent and the paper no longer light-sensitive.

Magnifying lens

Lightbox

Checking the negative for dirt and scratches

EXAMINING NEGATIVES
Negatives are extremely fragile and scratch easily. They also attract dust and dirt. Any such imperfections are magnified greatly when the image is blown up into a large-format print. For this reason, negatives are stored in transparent sleeves and only handled when necessary. They are examined under a magnifying lens on a lightbox and carefully cleaned before being used to make prints.

Instant pictures

THE FRUSTRATING WAIT between taking a photograph and seeing the result is something that has dogged photography from its very early days. Processing film and making prints takes time, so there has always been a demand for some kind of instant process. During the 19th century, there were many ingenious but short-lived systems that incorporated both a camera and a processing unit. But it was Edwin Land, the founder of Polaroid, who in 1948 launched the first camera capable of producing almost instant pictures. The first Polaroid camera used a peel-apart process. In 1972, the new SX-70 Polaroid camera produced one-sheet photos. Instant pictures took off. For the next 20 years, they were everywhere – at parties, at family celebrations, and on vacations. They even featured in work by modern artists.

Peel-apart Polaroid

FULFILLING A WISH
The idea for instant pictures came to Edwin Land (1909–91) in 1944 when his daughter asked why she had to wait to see the photograph he had just taken of her. Four years later, he launched the first Polaroid camera, using a self-portrait to show how the peel-apart process worked.

Print and negative paper rolls sit inside camera

Pop-up viewfinder

Folding lens and bellows unit

READY IN A MINUTE
The Model 95 (1948) was Polaroid's first instant-picture camera. After taking a picture, you pulled a sheet out of the camera, waited a minute while processing took place, then peeled away the top layer to reveal the image. Pictures were black and white at first – color did not arrive until 1963. Peel-apart Polaroids are still used by studio photographers to make sure that they are happy with the lighting and composition (see p. 32).

Credit-card-sized instant photo

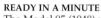

INSTANT MINI PHOTOS
Although digital cameras are taking over from instant film, they cannot yet produce instant color prints – at least not without being connected to a printer (see p. 19). Convinced that there was still a demand for instant pictures, in 1998 Fuji launched a new instant-photo film called Instax and a year later added a miniature version of it. Instax Mini point-and-shoot cameras fit easily in the palm of the hand and produce credit-card-sized instant pictures.

Collapsible fixed-focus lens

DOUBLE EXPOSURE
Part of China since 1950, Tibet is a remote, mountainous country. Until recently, many of its people had no experience of technologies taken for granted in the West. These two young Buddhist monks hold up pictures of themselves, shot by a visiting photographer with a Polaroid camera. They were astonished by the pictures – the first photos of themselves they had ever seen.

Latent image becomes visible

*Folding
viewfinder*

*Screen for
viewing picture*

SPEEDY PORTRAITS

Today, many people's experience of instant prints is the photo booth, used primarily for passport and ID card photographs. Digital technology has transformed these machines from a hit-and-miss experience into a more sophisticated photo-session. Customers can select from a choice of backgrounds before adopting a pose for the camera. As soon as the picture has been taken, they review the image on a color screen before deciding whether to print the photo or pose again for another shot.

*Processing unit
delivers prints here*

COLOR SNAPS IN A FLASH

In 1972, Polaroid introduced the SX-70, the first camera to produce one-sheet instant prints. There was nothing to peel away. After each picture was taken, the camera automatically ejected stiff white cards. These simply developed by themselves and turned, as if by magic, into full-color photographs. Before and after use, the camera folded flat.

POLAROID ART

Artists have always been attracted to Polaroids, especially those who discovered it is possible to manipulate the one-sheet photograph while it is developing and while the emulsions are still fluid. By rubbing or scratching the surface, the emulsions can be moved around beneath the plastic top sheet to create stretched, blurred, or paintlike effects. Far from frowning on such activities, Polaroid has encouraged artists to experiment with the medium.

*Pictures
are ready
in minutes*

*Hard-edged
tools for
rubbing and
scratching*

*Image distortion
during developing*

*Final image appears after
about three minutes*

Image darkens

*Colors become
more saturated*

HOW AN INSTANT PHOTO DEVELOPS

A Polaroid photograph is actually a multi-layered "sandwich" of light-sensitive film emulsions, developing chemicals, and colored dyes. When the exposed print comes out of the camera, it is squeezed through rollers to activate chemicals that stop any further exposure from taking place and start the development process. Colored dyes rise through the layers to the surface of the print to form the final image.

*Removing exposed
one-sheet print
from camera*

In the studio

Flash meter

Flexible bellows

Monorail

Lens-and-shutter unit

Sheet film carrier

WORKING IN THE STUDIO is all about being in control – whether the subject of the photograph is a fashion supermodel, a dish of beautifully prepared food, or a new car. Outdoors, too many factors are unpredictable – the weather, the light, the background, passers-by, and countless other possible distractions. In a studio, however, the photographer can take charge of the environment. The most important factor is the lighting. Professional photographers work with a range of lights, experimenting with the positioning and the quality of the setup until they achieve the effect they want. Usually, at least two lights are used: a "key" or principal light source, and a second "fill" light to lighten shadows created by the first. A variety of accessories such as diffusers, reflectors, umbrellas, hoods, and filters are then used to give precise control over the strength, quality, and color of the light.

MEDIUM-FORMAT STUDIO CAMERA
Cameras such as this modern medium-format Horseman are designed primarily for studio work. The lens-and-shutter unit at the front is joined by flexible bellows to the removable film or digital back, attached at the rear. Both slide back and forth on a monorail, and each can be raised, lowered, rotated, and tilted to give the photographer maximum control over focusing and perspective.

Backgrounds can be added later on computer

Umbrella in front of flash unit acts as reflector or diffuser

A CHANGE OF SCENE
Using digital imaging software, it is possible to change a background or insert a figure into a new setting (see p. 63). The result will be more convincing if the different images are shot from the same point of view and share the same lighting direction and quality. This is a good match, since both the figure and the room were shot from a similar low angle.

PREPARATION AND LIGHTING
While the photographer checks the lighting with a meter, the makeup artist examines her work under the bright studio lights and corrects any imperfections. Studio flash lights are much more powerful than ordinary lights, enabling the photographer to set the smallest aperture and so work with the largest possible area in focus (see p. 26). However, a bare studio flash is a particularly harsh, direct light source, so accessories such as umbrellas, softboxes, dishes, and snoots are needed to soften or reflect it.

Rolls of colored background paper

Test shot

Peel-apart negative layer

Underexposed

Overexposed

TAKING POLAROID TEST SHOTS
Few medium- and large-format cameras have automatic exposure metering. For this reason, photographers often fit a special Polaroid back and take several test shots to check the exposure and to preview the effect of their lighting setup when the flash is fired. This method is still used, but most people now prefer to see digital previews on a computer screen.

Conical attachment, known as a snoot, fits over flash unit to funnel light into narrow beam

Roll of backdrop paper forms continuous background and foreground

Makeup artist adds final touches

Photographer calculates exposure using a flash meter to measure the amount of light falling on subject when flash units fire

Dome-shaped structure, known as a softbox, fits over flash unit to diffuse the light and soften shadows

Picture can be previewed on screen – and shutter can even be fired from keyboard

Dish reflector controls spread of light from flash unit

35-mm digital SLR camera with image output connected to computer

Heavy-duty studio boom used as alternative to standard tripod

Lenses can be changed for different types of shot, such as close-ups or portraits

Freezing the moment

T HE WORLD IS FULL of creatures and objects that move too fast and events that happen too quickly for us to see clearly – birds in flight, a pouncing cat, falling raindrops, flashes of lightning, and so on. But photography can freeze time and capture images of these moments. Even a reasonable 35-mm or digital camera will probably have a fastest shutter speed of at least 1/2,000th second, swift enough to reduce blur in most moving subjects. However, most of the pictures shown here require special equipment and techniques. All high-speed photographers face two challenges: the first is to make the exposure very brief; the second is to time the exposure so that it takes place at precisely the right moment. Flash is the answer to the first problem, and an automatic triggering system is the solution to the second.

ILLUMINATING MOVEMENT
Eadweard Muybridge (1830–1904) was an early pioneer of high-speed photography. An Englishman who worked in the United States, he experimented with multi-camera setups and fast shutter speeds to photograph thousands of stop-motion sequences that analyzed how humans and animals move. Here, he is lecturing at the Royal Society in London in 1889.

Shutter unit in gun barrel

"Shooting" with a gun camera

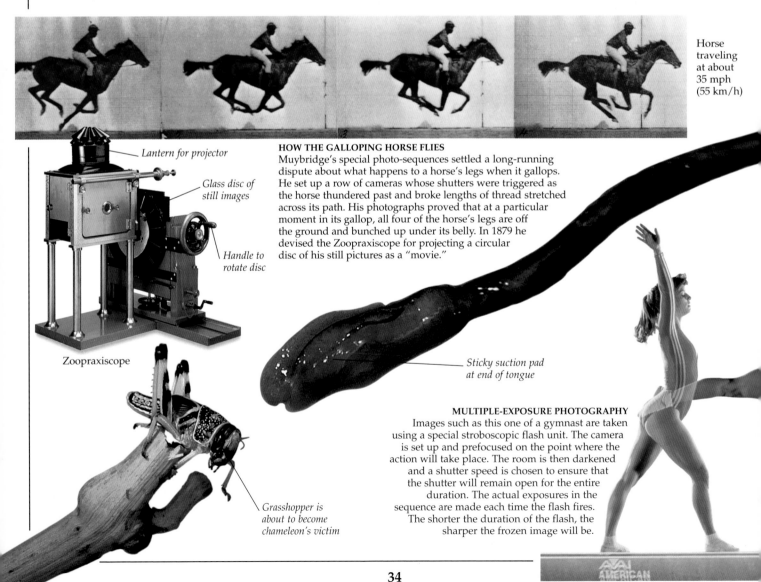

Horse traveling at about 35 mph (55 km/h)

Lantern for projector

Glass disc of still images

Handle to rotate disc

Zoopraxiscope

HOW THE GALLOPING HORSE FLIES
Muybridge's special photo-sequences settled a long-running dispute about what happens to a horse's legs when it gallops. He set up a row of cameras whose shutters were triggered as the horse thundered past and broke lengths of thread stretched across its path. His photographs proved that at a particular moment in its gallop, all four of the horse's legs are off the ground and bunched up under its belly. In 1879 he devised the Zoopraxiscope for projecting a circular disc of his still pictures as a "movie."

Sticky suction pad at end of tongue

MULTIPLE-EXPOSURE PHOTOGRAPHY
Images such as this one of a gymnast are taken using a special stroboscopic flash unit. The camera is set up and prefocused on the point where the action will take place. The room is then darkened and a shutter speed is chosen to ensure that the shutter will remain open for the entire duration. The actual exposures in the sequence are made each time the flash fires. The shorter the duration of the flash, the sharper the frozen image will be.

Grasshopper is about to become chameleon's victim

Wooden rifle stock makes it easier to hold the camera steady

TAKE AIM AND FIRE

Inspired by Muybridge's work, in 1881, French physiology professor Etienne Jules Marey (1830–1903) developed a rifle-shaped camera to photograph birds in flight. Loading his gun camera with circular glass photographic plates, he could record 12 shots of a flying bird in a single second. This English version, made in 1885, works in the same way. Marey called his photo-sequences chronophotographs. He later pioneered the use of multiple exposures to record a series of overlapping images of the same subject on a single photographic plate.

Chameleons project their tongues up to twice their body length

Hummingbird wings "frozen" in flight

SPLIT-SECOND TIMING

The panther chameleon's tongue darts out to catch its prey in just 1/16th of a second. A hummingbird's wings beat at a speed of up to 80 times every second. To the human eye, both movements register as nothing more than a blur, but a camera's fast shutter speed can capture a photographic image that freezes the motion in time.

MOMENT OF IMPACT

This shot of a bullet passing through an apple was taken with an exposure time of 1/3rd microsecond – that's just 1/3,000,000th of a second. The bullet was traveling at about 1,400 ft (450 m) per second. It was photographed by Harold "Doc" Edgerton (1904–90), a professor at the Massachusetts Institute of Technology who pioneered strobe flash and ultra-high-speed photography. The exposure would have been triggered by an automatic audio sensor that picked up the sound of the gun being fired.

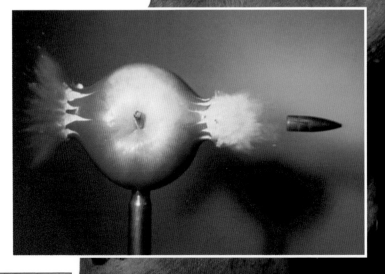

The world in close-up

PHOTOGRAPHING A SUBJECT CLOSE-UP reveals intriguing details we often overlook or are unable to see with the naked eye. It is hardly surprising, then, that the art of taking pictures at larger-than-life size is as old as photography itself. Today, it's fairly easy to equip cameras with close-up lenses or bellows units to get shots that are life-size or magnified by up to about 20 times. This type of photography is usually called macrophotography. To see closer than that, cameras need to be installed in an optical microscope. Photomicrography, as this is called, magnifies objects by as much as 2,000 times. But to capture images of the world of living cells or proteins we must use a scanning electron microscope, which relies on electron beams instead of light to produce a photolike image.

BOTANICAL STUDY
Anna Atkins was a British botanist and photographer who specialized in detailed, close-up images of ferns, grasses, and seaweeds. Her books were among the first to use photographic illustrations. This photogram (see p. 10) from 1853 is a cyanotype. Its Prussian blue tone comes from the chemicals used in making the print.

Bellows unit

Tripod handle

FLIGHT OF THE HONEY BEE
A bee laden with pollen is photographed with a macro lens at the moment of take-off. This is the most difficult type of close-up photography. Flash allows a shutter speed fast enough to freeze the bee in motion, but at such a close distance, accurate focusing is critical in order to get a sharp image of the subject.

Camera

Photographic viewfinder

Binoculars for viewing specimen

Ringflash

Blood vessels under a microscope

Six microscope lenses

Object of focus

SEEING THE PARTS OF A FLOWER
A bellows unit is the best solution for taking macro close-ups, such as of this yellow gerbera flower. It fits between the camera body and the lens and allows the lens to be moved farther away from the film, thus increasing magnification. For the best results, it is used with a tripod to keep it still during long exposures and a ringflash fitted around the lens to give even, shadow-free lighting.

MICROSCOPIC DETAIL
Photographs of the view through a microscope can be taken using a special camera setup. At the top, the camera is attached to a focusing unit that has its own viewfinder. Below it are the binocular eyepieces for viewing the specimen, and a cluster of six lenses giving a choice of magnification. The specimen is mounted on a flat slide, set in place on the specimen table, and lit from below. Sometimes filters are used to polarize or alter the color of the light.

Specimen table

Light source

Electron beam generator

Magnified image displayed on monitor

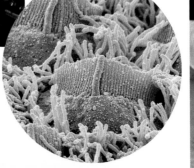
False-color SEM image of blood cells

EXPLORING THE HUMAN BODY
SEM images have revolutionized the way we see and think of our own bodies. They allow us to see beyond the limits of visible light and produce images at magnifications of many thousands of times. Usually, the initial images are in black and white. False color is added digitally to make the images easier to read. In the SEM shown at left, yellow is used for white blood cells, pink for the platelets that trigger blood clotting, and red for the red blood cells.

ELECTRON BEAMS BRING THE MINISCULE TO LIFE
Scanning electron microscopes (SEMs) are capable of far greater levels of magnification than optical microscopes. Strictly speaking, they do not use light. Instead, they "see" by firing a beam of electrons at an object. The electrons are focused into a very narrow beam, just like a light wave, which is scanned over the surface of a specimen. The specimen's electrons then create a current, or electrical signal. This signal is amplified and produces a photolike image with an exceptional depth of field on a computer screen.

False-color SEM image of tiny hair cells in the inner ear

WORLD'S SMALLEST BOOK
An SEM image of a millipede with the tiniest published book in the world. Made in Germany by typographer Joshua Reichert, it is no larger than the head of a match. This leather-bound, A–Z picture book has just 24 pages, each measuring a mere 0.09 x 0.11 in (2.4 x 2.9 mm).

Head lice are unable to jump – they can only grip

Strand of human hair

CLOSE ENCOUNTER WITH A HEAD LOUSE
The electron microscope can produce images with an astonishing 3-D quality – as this magnification of a head louse climbing a single strand of human hair demonstrates. It would be impossible to capture an image like this with a conventional microscope, which requires specimens to be mounted on glass slides. But there are drawbacks – the subject does have to be dead, fixed chemically, and sealed in a vacuum chamber.

Panoramic pictures

T HE VERY EARLIEST panoramic photographs were made by gluing together a series of overlapping images taken by moving, or panning, the camera slightly after each shot. Fox Talbot, the inventor of the calotype process, was one of the pioneers to make pictures in this way during the 1840s. However, he and others soon realized the benefits of a camera that could be rotated during the exposure to produce a single, long negative – initially on a curved glass plate. The specialist panoramic cameras that began to appear were of two kinds: either the whole camera panned around or the camera stayed still and only the lens rotated. Today, digital photography has brought panoramic pictures back into fashion. Software such as Photoshop has made it possible to join, or "stitch," multiple images together without scissors and glue.

Curved glass plate

A NEW TWIST
In 1859, Englishman Thomas Sutton invented a panoramic camera that used a unique, spherical, wide-angle lens that was filled with water. Sutton also created specially curved wet-collodion, glass plates for recording the images. These four negatives, each measuring 10 x 5 in (25 x 13 cm), are among the handful that still survive.

TRADING FLOOR IN A SINGLE SHOT
This is a shot of dealers in action at the Chicago Mercantile Exchange. It was taken with a special panoramic camera, a Fuji 617, so called because its negatives or transparencies measure 6 cm (or 2.4 in) high and 17 cm (or 6.8 in) wide. The camera is manual and has a direct viewfinder instead of reflex mirrors. This means that the lens can be positioned closer to the film for a wider angle of view. This can make horizontals at the top and bottom of the picture look curved – typical of many panoramas.

Complete camera assembly rotates

WORLD IN A SPIN
This Swiss-made Roundshot rotating camera is designed to be hand-held above the photographer's head, making it easy to take 360-degree panoramic pictures. It can swing around in a circle in less than a second. Most panoramic cameras need to be used with a tripod to keep the horizon level and the camera steady during longer exposures. Photographers using them walk around behind the camera lens as it rotates to avoid appearing in the picture.

Display shows shutter speed shooting angle, and film type

VERTICAL CHALLENGE
There is no reason why a panoramic camera cannot be turned onto its side and used to take vertical shots. In fact, the powerful slanting verticals that this creates tend to emphasize or exaggerate height – ideal for this shot of the John Hancock Building in Boston.

Panorama of English fishing port, 1913

THE WIDER PICTURE
The Russian Horizon swing-lens camera has a lens that rotates while the camera remains still. It uses 35-mm film, but produces a larger-than-normal negative or transparency – 58 mm wide instead of 35 mm. The pictures it takes therefore have a 120-degree angle of view. Exposure is controlled by adjusting the aperture of the lens and the speed at which it swings around.

Wide-angle viewfinder

EARLY PANORAMAS
This Pantascopic camera was built by two Englishmen, John Johnson and John Harrison, in 1862. It was wound up with a clockwork motor, then allowed to slowly rotate as a string-and-pulley system pulled a wet-collodion plate at the same speed past an exposing slot situated behind the lens. The exposed glass plate measured 7.5 x 12 in (19 x 30 cm) and captured panoramic images that had a 110-degree angle of view. Alfred Hind Robinson took his panoramic photograph of Whitby Bay, Yorkshire, England (above) some 50 years later.

Camera rotates on a circular base

The larger the overlap, the better

Upright shots have less perspective distortion

DIGITAL PANORAMAS
"Stitching" describes how digital imaging software can be used to combine separate photos into one panoramic view. It works best with shots that generously overlap one another and keep the horizon on the same level. The software overlays the images and will then do its best to disguise the seams. Some applications will compress or stretch areas of the image to force a fit. Others will try to correct perspective. Here, five separate shots showing visitors at a popular beauty spot have been combined to create one seamless image.

Photojournalism

DOCUMENTING HARDSHIP
Photographer Dorothea Lange documented the Great Depression in the 1930s. Her photographs brought to public attention the suffering of the displaced "Okie" farmers whose homesteads had been destroyed by the dust bowl that spread across the Midwest. Bleak images such as this inspired John Steinbeck's great novel *The Grapes of Wrath*.

IT HAS BEEN CLAIMED THAT photojournalism was born in January 1904, when the British *Daily Mirror* became the first newspaper to be illustrated with photographs throughout. Before that date, newspapers had mostly used engravings, which were easier to reproduce than photographs. In the following years, the work of documentary photographers found an outlet in print. In Germany in the 1920s and 1930s, picture editors began publishing collections of related images, and the picture essay emerged. Popular illustrated magazines followed – *Life*, one of the best-known, had a readership of more than 30 million per issue at its height. Today, a photojournalist's picture can be beamed electronically around the world in seconds. Photos of important events are broadcast on television and viewed on the Internet as they take place – and published in newspapers soon afterward.

The express train from Normandy fails to stop

SLR camera with wide-angle lens

GETTING THE SHOT
Photojournalists have to balance traveling light with having all the equipment they need. Most will always carry two cameras, one with a fast zoom or telephoto lens and the other with a wide-angle lens. These days, cameras are likely to be digital SLRs.

PHOTO-OPPORTUNISM
At the Gare Montparnasse in Paris in 1895, this train overran the buffers, plowed across the first-floor station concourse, and then crashed down into the street below. An unknown photographer clearly recognized a picture opportunity when he saw one – posters of his photograph are still sold today, more than 100 years later.

Telephoto lens for long-distance shots

A wall of motor-driven cameras and staring lenses

THE RISE OF THE PAPARAZZI
Diana, Princess of Wales, was perhaps the most photographed woman of all time. Pursued constantly, her life epitomized the cult of the celebrity. Paparazzi photographers, fueled by the willingness of the press to pay for intrusive pictures of famous people, now go to extreme lengths to secure candid, often embarrassing, photographs of the stars. Faster film, digital cameras, and powerful long lenses have helped them in the pursuit of their prey. The term "paparazzi" comes from the character Paparazzo, a photographer in Federico Fellini's movie *La Dolce Vita*.

A MOMENT IN HISTORY

All photojournalists are on the lookout for the one shot that perfectly reflects a mood, sums up a moment, or captures an important historic event. In this picture, an American soldier watches as a statue of former Iraqi leader Saddam Hussein is toppled to the ground in central Baghdad in April 2003. The shot takes advantage of some clever framing.

A 1961 issue of Look, *the US photo magazine*

The Daily Mirror, the first photographic newspaper

IMAGES FROM A WAR ZONE

The Vietnam War (1964–75) broke new ground in photojournalism. Never before had photographers been allowed such free access to combat zones, and the result was an intensively photographed conflict. Many of the most harrowing pictures – by photographers such as Larry Burrows, Tim Page, and Don McCullin – became symbolic images that fueled the anti-war movement in the United States and elsewhere.

THE NEWS IN PICTURES

Photographs in newspapers began to appear soon after the beginning of the 20th century, quickly taking the place of engravings. The 1940s and 1950s were the glory days of picture magazines such as *Life*, *Look*, *Picture Post*, and *Paris Match*. They reigned supreme until the arrival of television in the 1960s.

THE FALL OF THE BERLIN WALL

When the wall separating East and West Berlin fell in November 1989, it marked the end of the Cold War and was celebrated by a mass public uprising. Photojournalists from all over the world were on hand to record the event. This shot shows young Berliners sitting triumphantly astride the top of the graffiti-covered wall. It stands in stark contrast to the images of a bleak, empty no-man's land fenced with barbed wire that had marked the preceding 28 years.

Extreme photography

LOOKING AT A PHOTOGRAPH OR A VIDEO is as close as most people get to climbing a Himalayan peak, trekking to the South Pole, skydiving from an airplane, or peering over the rim of a volcano. Photographers must be our eyes. They bring us images from the world's hottest, coldest, wettest, highest, and most dangerous places. In the 19th century, the first travel photographers were pioneers, struggling with bulky cameras and makeshift traveling darkrooms. It could take weeks before their pictures went on public view. Today's outdoor and extreme sports photographers are more likely to be equipped with digital SLRs, a laptop computer, and a satellite telephone. Their pictures can be beamed from one side of the world to another and be up on a web page within moments.

HANGING BY A THREAD
The only way to get close-up shots of climbers in action is to climb with them. For obvious reasons, the cameras used are as small and lightweight as possible. Here, two climbers photograph each other while suspended from an overhang on the mile-high north face of Trango Tower in Pakistan.

Altimeter displays height above ground and warns when to release parachute

POLAR CONDITIONS
In Antarctica during the winter, temperatures rarely rise above −40°F (−40°C). In such conditions, camera electronics may malfunction, batteries may fail, and film becomes brittle. There is even a danger of getting frostbite while changing lenses or looking through the viewfinder. On the positive side, wildlife in this remote region is unused to the presence of humans and therefore less likely to be camera-shy.

Emperor penguin

HEAD FOR HEIGHTS
When skydiving, there is little time for experimenting with camera angles or trying out different compositions. Even a jump from 16,000 ft (4,900 m) – the highest possible without using oxygen – will give only about 75 seconds of free fall before the parachute must be released. Skydivers need to keep both hands free, so mounting cameras onto a fiberglass helmet is the solution for most photographers. One, two, or even three can be attached at the same time – still cameras as well as video camcorders. A special eyepiece can be pulled down to act as a remote viewfinder.

Video camera

35-mm SLR camera mounted upside down

Eyepiece for framing

Head-mounted cameras

Skydiver free-falls at speeds of more than 120 mph (190 km/h)

AN EYE ON THE STORM
Photographers who specialize in taking pictures of tornadoes and other severe weather conditions are called "storm-chasers." They track the development of storms with information from remote weather satellites, and can drive hundreds of miles in a day to be in the right place when the storm reaches its peak. Tornadoes can have wind speeds of up to 300 mph (500 km/h), so it's safest to photograph one as it moves away.

Volcano erupts, sending up a fountain of lava

Heat-resistant body suit

HEAT OF THE MOMENT
Two of the world's largest volcanoes, Mauna Loa and Kilauea (left) are on the island of Hawaii. Both are active, and erupt regularly. Volcanologists wanting to take samples of the gas and molten lava must brave intense heat and the danger of further tremors. They wear special protective suits with a metal coating that reflects heat and helps them stay cool. Of course, photographers looking for close-up shots of the eruptions and lava flows run the same risks and must be similarly protected.

The view from up there

ALMOST AS SOON AS cameras were invented, photographers seemed eager to get them up in the air to take pictures of the world from above. Hot-air balloons were among the first airborne craft to provide photographers with a lift. But when the Wright Brothers invented powered flight in 1903, aerial photography really took off. It was also about this time that lenses with better optics appeared, so cameras were soon being used in map-making – as they have been ever since. Today, aerial photography covers a wide range of applications. Inexpensive cameras are attached to model airplanes or kites using basic homemade devices, while the sophisticated modern technology of imaging systems is carried by high-altitude spy planes and by satellites orbiting Earth.

UP AND AWAY
In 1853, French caricaturist Felix Nadar took up photography. Just six years later, he opened one of the largest portrait studios in Paris and became a well-known celebrity photographer. In 1858, he combined photography with another of his passions – hot-air ballooning. Undaunted by the problems of having to prepare collodion wet plates in a darkened balloon basket, he became the first person to take photographs from the air.

EYE IN THE SKY
The US military aircraft *Global Hawk* is the world's most sophisticated high-altitude spy plane. Uncrewed and remotely piloted from the ground by computer, it can fly nonstop 24-hour missions and capture detailed radar, infrared, and black-and-white images of an area of about 11,600 sq miles (30,000 sq km). Its digital cameras and other electronic sensing devices are sensitive enough to spot a life raft in the ocean from an altitude of more than 60,000 ft (18,000 m).

HOW THE LAND LIES
This vertical aerial shot shows the Leeds and Liverpool Canal near Steeton, England. The time of day is an important factor in aerial photography. In early morning or before dusk, when the sun is low in the sky, it casts long shadows that highlight features in the landscape. Aerial shots taken at these times can therefore sometimes reveal archaeological remains, such as ancient earthworks, that would otherwise be invisible. At midday, when the sun is directly overhead, there are few shadows and finer details can be recorded.

Camera controls and electronics

Floor mount

Optics by Carl Zeiss

Eight camera lenses

MAPPING THE LANDSCAPE
A high-precision mapping camera is fixed to the floor of the aircraft that carries it and shoots vertically downward. By capturing overlapping images and using a mixture of optical and infrared sensors, it can obtain very accurate data about distances between particular points, terrain height, geology, land use, and even the health of vegetation. This digital mapping camera unit contains eight different camera lenses and image sensors.

1. AMERICA BY SATELLITE

Satellites are constantly sending pictures of Earth from space to help scientists monitor the weather. Geostationary satellites are positioned 21,600 miles (36,000 km) above the equator, and take pictures of Earth beneath them. Polar-orbiting satellites, on the other hand, circle the globe capturing images of the areas over which they fly.

Individual buildings are visible

Spy-plane photo of a chemical plant in Sudan

2. SPACE SHUTTLE RADAR

This high-altitude aerial picture of the New York City area was taken from the Space Shuttle *Endeavour*'s Imaging Radar system (SIR-C). Because radar can penetrate clouds, it's able to capture images in any weather. Pictures are initially black and white. Different radar channels are then allocated certain colors. Water is black; light blue or red areas are dense urban developments.

Long Island Sound

3. FROM THE INTERNATIONAL SPACE STATION

Streets, buildings, parks, piers, and bridges on Manhattan Island are now clearly visible from an altitude of about 240 miles (385 km). This shot was taken with a digital camera and 800-mm lens by the crew aboard the International Space Station Alpha, orbiting the earth at a speed of about 17,500 mph (28,000 km/h).

Bird's-eye view of Pigeon Point Lighthouse, California

4. NEW YORK FROM A HELICOPTER

This shot of Manhattan Island was taken from a helicopter. It's known as an oblique shot to distinguish it from vertical photographs, which are taken looking straight down at the ground. At this altitude, 35-mm film cameras or digital SLRs are used. But photographing from planes at higher altitudes requires specialist cameras, often equipped with large wire-frame viewfinders, handgrips, and oversized controls so they can be operated while wearing gloves.

Harness for kite camera

Rotate mechanism

FM radio receiver

Radio-controlled shutter "finger"

KITE CAMERA HARNESSES

Cameras attached to kites can be used to take effective low-altitude aerial photographs. This home-made harness held the Yashica compact 35-mm camera that captured this shot of Pigeon Point Lighthouse. The harness includes a radio receiver so that the camera can be rotated and tilted, and its shutter fired, by remote control from the ground.

Focus on infinity

AN ASTRONOMICAL INVENTION
In 1857, the British astronomer Warren De La Rue adapted a collodion camera (see p. 11), attached it to a telescope, and created what he called a "photoheliograph" to take some of the first photographs of the Sun, Moon, and planets. In 1860, he shipped the device to Rivabellosa in northern Spain and erected this makeshift observatory to photograph a total solar eclipse.

Detachable film magazine – the part that came back to earth

PHOTOGRAPHY HAS ALWAYS played an important part in our understanding of how the universe works. Although telescopes help us to see far beyond the limits of the naked eye, on their own they are still limited. But attach a camera to a telescope, and suddenly we can see so much more. Using sensitive film (or digital sensors) and long exposure times, details are revealed that would otherwise be invisible. Indeed, 19th-century astronomers working with the first astronomical cameras were astonished to discover that outer space was much more crowded than they had thought. Their first photographs of the night sky showed it to be full of hitherto unknown stars, galaxies, and constellations. Space travel was a further breakthrough. Once cameras were taken on board rockets, orbiting satellites, and space probes, they saw the universe clearly for the first time, undistorted by Earth's atmosphere.

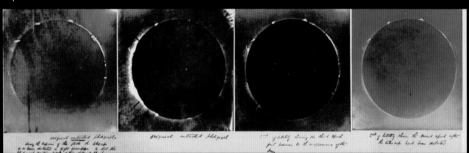

TOTAL ECLIPSE OF THE SUN
De La Rue's photographs of the solar eclipse in 1860 represented a scientific breakthrough. For the first time, there was documentary evidence that solar flares really existed. They had been observed by astronomers many times before, but it had never been proven that they come from the surface of the Sun. Until photography settled the debate, many had argued that they were merely optical illusions caused by the atmosphere.

Astrotelescope

35-mm camera in place of eyepiece

Craters on the Moon photographed from Earth

THE SKY AT NIGHT
One of the problems with photographing the night sky is that stars and planets do not stand still. They move across the sky as Earth rotates. This has the effect of creating light trails when using the long exposures that may be necessary. To avoid this, scientists attach the telescope to a special mount that has a slow-motion drive that pans the telescope against Earth's rotation. This freezes the movement of objects in the sky, as if Earth were standing still.

GREAT BALL OF FIRE
Solar flares are huge explosions of superheated plasma or ionized gas that erupt into space from the Sun's atmosphere. The Solar and Heliospheric Observatory (SOHO) is just one of the orbiting satellites that monitors and photographs the Sun's activity constantly. This picture was taken with SOHO's extreme ultraviolet imaging telescope.

Hasselblad
SWC

*Radio antenna sends
pictures back to Earth*

*Aperture door opens to
admit incoming light rays*

FIRST CAMERAS ON THE MOON

Neil Armstrong's picture of Buzz Aldrin's 1969 moonwalk
is perhaps the most famous photo of all time. It was shot
with one of several specially adapted Hasselblads that the
astronauts took with them – all designed to work in zero
gravity and at temperatures ranging from over 250°F (120°C)
in the sun to –85°F (–65°C) in the shade.

*Solar panels provide
power for the satellite*

LIGHT FANTASTIC

Pillarlike clouds of dust and gas
make up the Eagle Nebula, about
7,000 light-years from Earth. At the
tips of the "fingers" of cloud, new stars
are being formed. The blue halo effect is
caused by ultraviolet light from young,
hot stars evaporating unstable hydrogen
gases. This enhanced digital image was
created from data transmitted by the
sensors aboard the Hubble Space
Telescope, orbiting 370 miles (600 km)
above the surface of Earth.

VIEWS FROM HUBBLE

Launched in 1990, the
Hubble Space Telescope was
designed to capture images of
the universe that Earth's
atmosphere makes it impossible
to obtain from the ground. It is
loaded with optical, infrared, and
ultraviolet sensors. Unfortunately,
there was an initial fault with one
of the huge 8-ft- (2.4-m-) diameter
mirrors that make up the telescope,
and in 1993 astronauts were sent
up by space shuttle to repair it.
Since then, the pictures sent back
to Earth have been breathtaking.

Underwater photography

THE FIRST UNDERWATER PHOTOGRAPHS are said to have been taken by an Englishman named William Thompson. In 1856, he waterproofed a simple box camera, attached it to a pole, and lowered it beneath the waves off the coast of southern England. During the 10-minute exposure, the camera slowly flooded with seawater, but the picture survived. Underwater photography was born. Near the surface, where the water is clear and there is sufficient light, it is quite possible for an amateur photographer to take great shots with an inexpensive underwater camera. Most fish are naturally inquisitive and will swim quite close to people if they are not frightened away. At greater depths, where it is dark and cold, photography is the principal way of exploring a mysterious deep-sea world, 95 percent of which has never been seen before.

THE VIEW FROM BELOW
French naturalist Louis Boutan is responsible for the oldest surviving underwater photograph. It was shot in about 1893 using a bulky waterproof camera weighing almost 400 lb (180 kg), which he lowered to the seabed on the Mediterranean coast. His murky exposures lasted as long as 30 minutes each.

THE DIVERS' FAVORITE
The first Nikonos camera was made in 1963, after Nikon bought a small underwater-camera company founded by deep-sea explorer Jacques Cousteau. Nikonos cameras were specially built "amphibious" cameras. They have large controls that are easy to operate underwater. The cameras come with interchangeable lenses adapted for underwater work and a system of clip-on flash heads or "strobes." The Nikonos V, shown here, is the most recent model, launched in 1984.

Flash head or strobe unit

Focusing knob

Aperture setting knob

UP CLOSE AND PERSONAL
Great White sharks are among the world's most ferocious predators, and divers wishing to get close enough to photograph them need the protection of specially toughened steel cages. The sharks are lured to the camera with bait made from tuna heads and a mixture of chicken blood, oil, and fish called "burley."

Large shutter release lever

Easy-to-grip handle

WATERPROOF CAMERAS
Ordinary land cameras can be used underwater if placed inside watertight covers, or housings. The Nexus housing, shown left, is specially built for a Nikon digital SLR camera, allowing it to be taken down to a depth of 300 ft (100 m). It has large handles and controls, and a special viewfinder that allows it to be used by a mask-wearing diver. Waterproof disposable cameras are inexpensive and can be used while snorkeling or in a pool.

Using a disposable camera underwater

TALES FROM THE DEEP
This fanfin anglerfish lives at depths of up to 9,000 ft (3,000 m) underwater. There, the pressure is so great that normal amphibious cameras would implode and diving is out of the question. The only way to capture photographs of such deep-sea marine life is to go down in pressurized submersibles or to send remotely operated robot submarines. Uncrewed vehicles use sonar equipment to detect underwater creatures and trigger the camera or carry CCTV cameras that transmit signals to the surface so that the photographer can preview what the camera sees.

Lure emits light to attract prey

TURNING BLUE AND BLACK
This wreck being explored by divers in the Maldives is not deep, since colors are still discernible. If it were below about 60 ft (20 m), everything would look blue. This is because certain wavelengths of light are absorbed by water at different depths. Red and orange do not penetrate beyond about 15 ft (5 m). Next, yellows and greens are filtered out. Then only blue remains. Its brightness depends on the strength and position of the sun, and whether the surface of the water is smooth or choppy. Finally, there is no light at all.

SHOOTING FISH
The key to underwater photography is to get as close to the subject as possible. This is because light behaves differently underwater, and through a camera lens, objects appear larger than they do on the surface. It's dark underwater, too, so at depths of 100 ft (30 m), flash is essential. Flash heads should be positioned as close to the subject and as far to one side of the camera as possible or they will illuminate all the tiny particles and debris floating in the water, causing a snowstorm effect called "backscatter."

Photographing wildlife

TAKING SUCCESSFUL PHOTOGRAPHS of animals has more to do with understanding their behavior and knowing how to be in the right place at the right time than with technology and camera gadgets. Using the right equipment is important, however, and devices such as hides, special telephoto lenses, remote-control systems, tripods, and high-speed flash all help photographers achieve the pictures they want. But getting to know the animals – learning where they live, what they eat, and when and where they feed – is critical. Even the most timid and the most aggressive animals tend to be creatures of habit, and there is a pattern to their daily or seasonal activity that will be revealed by patient study and observation. For this reason, many professional wildlife photographers also have a background knowledge of natural history.

EARLY-EVENING REFRESHMENTS
In the Etosha National Park in Namibia, most activity takes place between dawn and 10 a.m., before the day becomes really hot, and between 4 p.m. and dusk, when temperatures begin to fall. This telephoto shot of zebras was taken as the sun was going down, at the time when they usually come to drink at a favorite water hole.

HIDE AND SEEK
Specially camouflaged hides can help conceal a photographer and his or her equipment. What is important is to set up the hide in advance of the shoot, and then to be patient on the day. Birds and animals will know that the hide is there, but they need to get used to it and to understand that it is not a threat.

A fast, quiet motor drive helps with concealed photography

Monarch butterfly

Each tripod leg can be angled separately

Professional digital SLR camera

Lens, rather than camera, is mounted on tripod

Lens hood minimizes glare from snow

CLOSING IN ON A SUBJECT
Tripods are essential for close-up work because they prevent the shaking that can occur if a camera is hand-held for a long exposure. A tripod with a swivel arm that lowers the camera to the ground is very useful for photographing flowers and insects that feed on them.

SO NEAR – AND YET SO FAR
The natural habitat of the polar bear is the Arctic, where the only practical mode of transportation may be a snowmobile. Temperatures can drop to –67°F (–55°C), at which point camera batteries can fail and zoom lenses may freeze solid. The bears can be dangerous, too, so a long telephoto lens allows the photographer to shoot from a safe distance.

Polar bear and cubs in Canadian Arctic

Fast shutter speed means wings can be photographed without motion blur

Canon
400-mm IS lens

IMPROVING LENS STABILITY
It is not always practical to use a tripod to steady a camera. This is why some modern lenses have built-in image-stabilization (IS) systems to minimize camera shake. Sensors in the lens detect wobbles and instruct internal mechanisms to compensate for the movement.

NOCTURNAL EXPOSURE
Food left as bait lured this fox into an upturned garbage can where a camera had been hidden. With the fox in position, the photographer took the shot from a distance using an electronic cable release – attached to the camera earlier – to fire the shutter. For longer distances, remote-control devices using infrared beams or wireless transmitters can be used. When the photographer is not present, a movement-sensor system can be set up so that the animal itself triggers the shutter.

Shots taken at five frames per second

Motor-driven sequence of exposures

City fox scavenging at night

Electronic cable release

WILDLIFE LOCATION SHOOT
The photographer wanted a shot of this hawk with its wings fully outstretched, about to launch itself into the air. The bird's handler felt the hawk would be more at ease if the shoot took place outdoors, which also meant there was no need to worry about studio lighting. The photographer decided not to use a tripod because he wanted to be able to move quickly – in any case, the fast shutter speed required to freeze the movement of the bird's wings ruled out the risk of any camera shake.

Lightweight 35-mm SLR allows freedom of movement

Professional handler directs bird's movement

Portable reflector bounces light onto underside of bird's wings

Tripod

Travel cases for carrying extra equipment

Images of the invisible

LIGHT, WHICH IS ESSENTIAL to photography, is a form of energy that travels in waves. Within a limited range, our eyes are able to distinguish different wavelengths, which we see as the colors of the rainbow, from red at one extreme through to violet at the other. This is how we view the world. But there are many other wavelengths of light which, although invisible to the human eye, can be "seen" and photographed by special cameras and image sensors. Infrared, ultraviolet, and X-rays are among the best known. Some of the imaging techniques shown here don't use light at all. A magnetic resonance imaging (MRI) scanner, for example, uses a combination of magnetism and radio waves to pick up signals from the human body that it sends to a computer to make into the kind of enhanced image we can recognize.

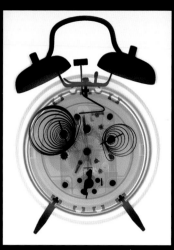

ILLUMINATING X-RAYS
Because X-rays have a shorter wavelength and more energy than visible light, they can pass through soft materials (such as fabrics and body tissue). However, they cannot penetrate solid objects such as metal and bone. Photographs made by exposing photographic film to X-rays are called radiographs. This colored radiograph of an alarm clock shows inner metal parts that would otherwise be invisible.

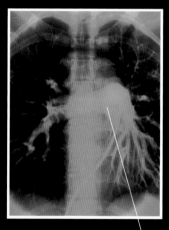

INFRARED VISION
Special infrared film and sensors are responsive to invisible infrared light. In this aerial photograph, trees and bushes appear red or pink. Such false-color images can reveal details that would not normally be seen. In fact, color infrared film was originally made to detect hidden military bases, because it would show up the difference between living foliage and dead branches cut for camouflage. It is also used by forensic scientists to spot forgeries in documents and paintings.

MRI scan shows soft tissues of brain

VEIN BEHAVIOR
An arteriogram (or angiogram) is a type of X-ray designed for taking photographs of veins and arteries. To "see" the veins, an opaque, colored dye is injected into the bloodstream. X-rays cannot pass through this dye, so once it has circulated, the X-ray image is taken. Here, the pulmonary arteries and veins in the lungs are shown in orange. The rib cage can be seen in blue.

Main pulmonary artery

Bone structure can be seen

GETTING INSIDE SOMEONE'S HEAD
Magnetic resonance imaging (MRI) uses magnets and radio waves to produce very detailed images. Inside an MRI scanner, exposure to a strong magnetic field aligns the hydrogen atoms in the body. Short pulses of radio waves then knock the atoms briefly out of alignment. A second magnet then detects the signals transmitted as the atoms realign once more. The data is sent from the scanner to a computer that processes it and turns it into a picture on a monitor screen. MRI scans are used for identifying abnormalities such as tumors, for examining the spine, and for diagnosing sports injuries.

HOW BEES SEE NECTAR

Nectar guides visible

Nectar guides invisible

Under ultraviolet (UV) light, the petals of a potentilla flower turn from yellow to blue and dark patches appear. These patches are "nectar guides" and are used by bees, whose eyes are sensitive to UV light. This type of light lies beyond the violet end of the spectrum (hence the name) and is invisible to the human eye. However, it can be seen by certain animals and is recorded on photographic film. It is often used for security marking or for detecting forgeries.

Cool areas appear blue

Warm areas appear red

Bubble trails left by pion particles

BUBBLING WITH LIFE

Atoms are made up of subatomic particles – electrons, protons, neutrons, neutrinos, muons, pions, and many more types. Subatomic particles are simply too small to see. But in a bubble chamber (below), the fast-moving particles create trails of bubbles in their wake. These are photographed through glass portholes, often with more than one camera. The black-and-white images are later artificially colored.

BUBBLE CHAMBER

The bubble chamber was invented to study the behavior of subatomic particles. It contains liquid hydrogen under high pressure kept just below its boiling point. When particles pass through the hydrogen, they cause it to boil, leaving trails of tiny bubbles that can be photographed.

THERMAL IMAGING

The heat given off by an object is transmitted in the form of "thermal" infrared light. The wavelength of this light is too long for us to see, but it can be picked up by cameras with special sensors that respond to thermal radiation. The process is called thermography and produces color images that can be viewed on a computer screen. In this image, the warmest areas appear red, and the coldest appear blue. Thermography is widely used in medical diagnosis (where it can help doctors detect cancers or circulatory disorders), as well as in secret surveillance and search-and-rescue operations.

Green from glowing phosphor screen

LIGHTING UP THE DARKNESS

Photographs such as this night shot of a ground crew on a US Navy carrier can be taken using special image intensifiers. These absorb the tiny amounts of light, including infrared, that are present and amplify them so that we can see the image. The amplification can be as much as 250,000 times the original light source. Image intensifiers have phosphor screens that cause images to appear green.

Spy cameras

ONE OF THE SPY'S MAIN TASKS is to obtain secret information, copy it, and pass it back to his or her controller. Before the days of copier machines, scanners, and electronic documents, a camera was the surest way to copy secret papers. Consequently, for much of the 20th century, the scientists of the world's top intelligence agencies vied with one another to invent ever more ingenious ways of miniaturizing and disguising cameras. Lenses were built into umbrellas, briefcases, and cigarette packs, and they were concealed in watches, books, pens, and radios. One manufacturer – Minox – is famous for making the sub-miniature cameras used by almost every spy who operated in the last 60 years.

Fixed-focus lens

Aperture control with yellow (bright) and blue (dim) settings

DO YOU HAVE THE TIME?
The Steineck ABC camera was made in Germany in 1949 by an inventor named Dr. Steiner. Disguised as a wristwatch, it could take six pictures on a special film disc – which spies found irritatingly difficult to load. Now, of course, miniaturized digital technology has replaced bulky film mechanisms, so spy cameras are even easier to disguise.

Pinhole

Clock face

UMBRELLA ATTACHMENT
This umbrella concealed a tiny spy camera known as the F21. It was adapted by the Russian KGB in 1948 from a German Robot camera. Built into the wooden handle, the camera fitted snugly inside the umbrella's outer casing. A small hole allowed the lens to peep through. Although it had no viewfinder, it could fire off several shots in quick succession.

Book concealment

Shutter release pressure plate

Opening for lens

Winder

Lens

F21 camera

Shutter release

Wooden block

Shutter release

Lens opening

MATCHBOX CAMERAS
During World War II, the US secret service commissioned Kodak to create a series of miniature 16-mm cameras that could be concealed inside matchboxes. They were disguised with labels from the country where they were to be used.

BETWEEN THE LINES
The Swiss-made Tessina camera was small enough to be concealed in a pack of cigarettes or between the covers of a book. It was the world's smallest motor-driven 35-mm camera and could take a series of 10 pictures before it needed rewinding. The camera lens looked out through a hole in the front edge of the book.

Prongs position camera to align with lens opening

YOU'VE BEEN FRAMED
This fake sunglasses case was designed by the East German Stasi (secret police) to conceal a tiny KGB Toychka camera. The lens looked through a mesh of small holes in the case and the camera was fired by pressing a lever on one side. A cut-in-half pair of sunglasses completed the illusion – convincing enough provided the sun did not shine.

Half a pair of sunglasses

Frame counter

Spring rod activates shutter

Lens

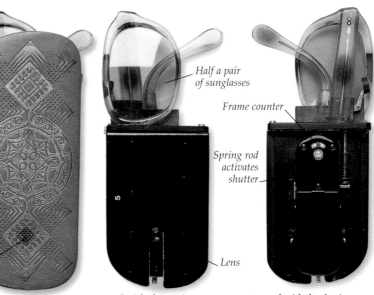

Mesh over lens

Opening in fabric for lens

Camera in case

Inside front view

Inside back view

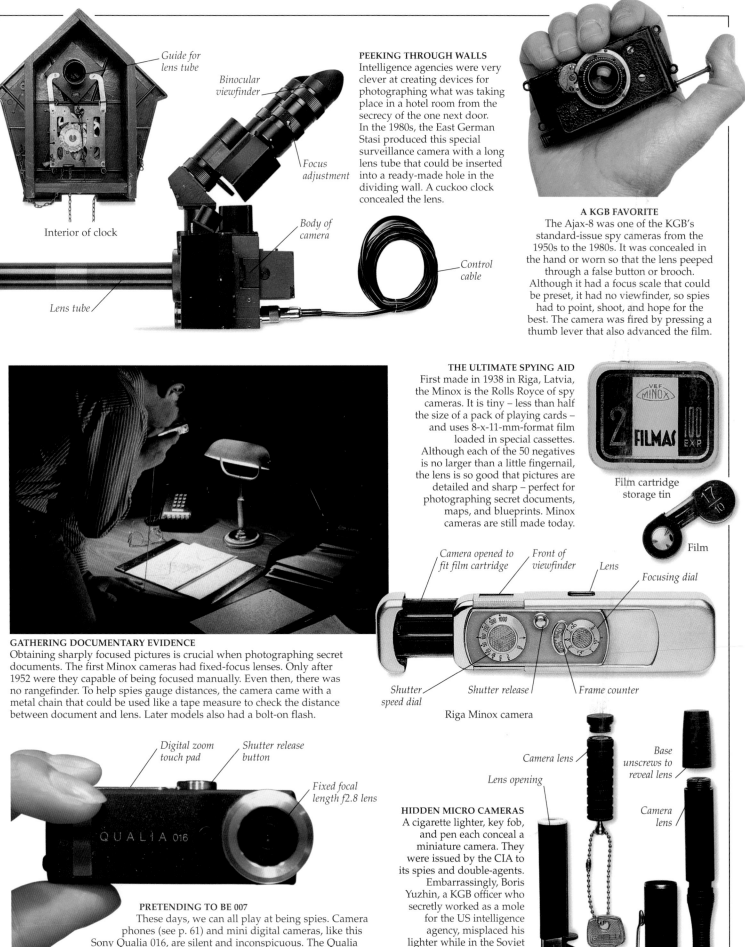

Guide for lens tube

Binocular viewfinder

Focus adjustment

Interior of clock

Body of camera

Control cable

Lens tube

PEEKING THROUGH WALLS

Intelligence agencies were very clever at creating devices for photographing what was taking place in a hotel room from the secrecy of the one next door. In the 1980s, the East German Stasi produced this special surveillance camera with a long lens tube that could be inserted into a ready-made hole in the dividing wall. A cuckoo clock concealed the lens.

A KGB FAVORITE

The Ajax-8 was one of the KGB's standard-issue spy cameras from the 1950s to the 1980s. It was concealed in the hand or worn so that the lens peeped through a false button or brooch. Although it had a focus scale that could be preset, it had no viewfinder, so spies had to point, shoot, and hope for the best. The camera was fired by pressing a thumb lever that also advanced the film.

THE ULTIMATE SPYING AID

First made in 1938 in Riga, Latvia, the Minox is the Rolls Royce of spy cameras. It is tiny – less than half the size of a pack of playing cards – and uses 8-x-11-mm-format film loaded in special cassettes. Although each of the 50 negatives is no larger than a little fingernail, the lens is so good that pictures are detailed and sharp – perfect for photographing secret documents, maps, and blueprints. Minox cameras are still made today.

Film cartridge storage tin

Film

GATHERING DOCUMENTARY EVIDENCE

Obtaining sharply focused pictures is crucial when photographing secret documents. The first Minox cameras had fixed-focus lenses. Only after 1952 were they capable of being focused manually. Even then, there was no rangefinder. To help spies gauge distances, the camera came with a metal chain that could be used like a tape measure to check the distance between document and lens. Later models also had a bolt-on flash.

Camera opened to fit film cartridge

Front of viewfinder

Lens

Focusing dial

Shutter speed dial

Shutter release

Frame counter

Riga Minox camera

Digital zoom touch pad

Shutter release button

Fixed focal length f2.8 lens

PRETENDING TO BE 007

These days, we can all play at being spies. Camera phones (see p. 61) and mini digital cameras, like this Sony Qualia 016, are silent and inconspicuous. The Qualia has a highly sophisticated imaging sensor, a tiny color LCD screen, and is about the same size as a cigarette lighter. Sony markets it in a James Bond–style black leather attaché case.

Camera lens

Lens opening

Base unscrews to reveal lens

Camera lens

HIDDEN MICRO CAMERAS

A cigarette lighter, key fob, and pen each conceal a miniature camera. They were issued by the CIA to its spies and double-agents. Embarrassingly, Boris Yuzhin, a KGB officer who secretly worked as a mole for the US intelligence agency, misplaced his lighter while in the Soviet Consulate in San Francisco in 1981. When it was found, the camera was discovered.

3-D photography

WE ARE ABLE TO SEE THREE dimensions (3-D) because each of our eyes views an object from a slightly different angle and produces a combined image with depth. Photographers have long been fascinated by ways of making this work with their images. Henry Fox Talbot experimented with 3-D photography in the 1840s, and by the 1850s there was a public craze for "stereo" images. In the Victorian home, a special viewer for stereo pictures was almost as common as a television set is today. Nowadays, most people's experience of 3-D photography involves 3-D pictures designed to be viewed with special glasses, or holograms. Holograms are created using lasers, which emit light waves of the same frequency that remain in phase with one another.

3-D PRIZEWINNER
The inventor of 3-D holography, Dr. Denis Gabor, came up with the idea in 1948. Remarkably, it was 14 more years before two Americans were able to employ newly discovered laser light to see whether or not his theory would actually work. Fortunately, it did – and Gabor was awarded the Nobel prize. He is immortalized here in a transmission hologram.

Laser

TRANSMISSION HOLOGRAM
All holograms are made using laser light. The laser beam is split in two so that one, the reference beam, is directed toward a holographic plate or piece of film. The other beam is reflected off the object, here a dinosaur, carrying with it information about the object's size, shape, and texture. The two beams then meet at the holographic plate, producing an interference pattern that records the 3-D information. The equipment must remain absolutely still – any vibration will disrupt the light waves and stop the image from being recorded.

Lenses expand beams onto mirrors

Beam splitter divides beam in two

One beam is reflected onto dinosaur, the other beam onto holographic plate

Object must remain motionless

Beam splitter

Lens

Mirror

Object stand

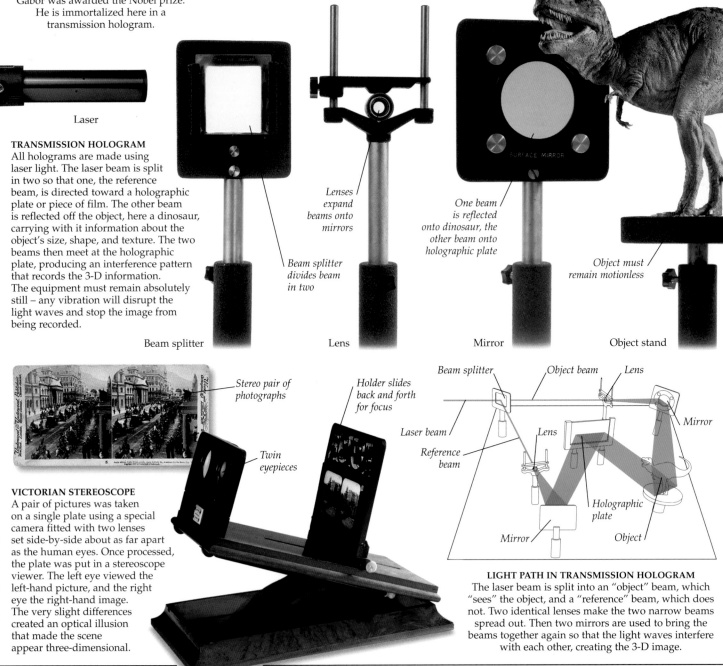

Stereo pair of photographs

Holder slides back and forth for focus

Twin eyepieces

VICTORIAN STEREOSCOPE
A pair of pictures was taken on a single plate using a special camera fitted with two lenses set side-by-side about as far apart as the human eyes. Once processed, the plate was put in a stereoscope viewer. The left eye viewed the left-hand picture, and the right eye the right-hand image. The very slight differences created an optical illusion that made the scene appear three-dimensional.

Beam splitter

Object beam

Lens

Laser beam

Reference beam

Lens

Mirror

Holographic plate

Mirror

Object

LIGHT PATH IN TRANSMISSION HOLOGRAM
The laser beam is split into an "object" beam, which "sees" the object, and a "reference" beam, which does not. Two identical lenses make the two narrow beams spread out. Then two mirrors are used to bring the beams together again so that the light waves interfere with each other, creating the 3-D image.

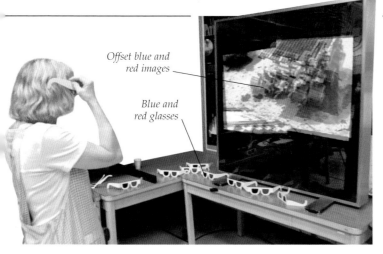

Offset blue and red images

Blue and red glasses

MASS-PRODUCED HOLOGRAMS
When the euro was introduced in 2002, 16 billion banknotes were issued, each featuring an embossed hologram. These are transmission holograms with a mirror backing and are the type most easily mass-produced at low cost. The areas of light and dark from the holographic plate are converted to a pattern of minute grooves embossed into sheets of thin foil, as shown here.

Checking quality of embossed holographic foil

SEEING THE WHOLE PICTURE
A stereo image can be created by duplicating a photograph and displaying one version in red slightly offset against a second version displayed in blue. When viewed through glasses with one red lens and one blue lens, the image appears in 3-D. This works on paper as well as on computer screens, as shown here. A similar technique is used to create hidden-picture stereograms.

Glass plate coated with photographic emulsion

Holographic plate

DOUBLE TROUBLE
When two 3-D images are recorded on the same holographic plate, or piece of film, the result is a double-channel transmission hologram. Here, a second 3-D image of the dinosaur's skeleton has been superimposed over the original 3-D image of the creature in all its fleshy glory. Each image is then assigned a different viewing angle. This means that the creature can be seen stripped down to its bare bones when viewed from the left (as here) and in the flesh when viewed from the right.

Holographic image has all the dimensions of the original object

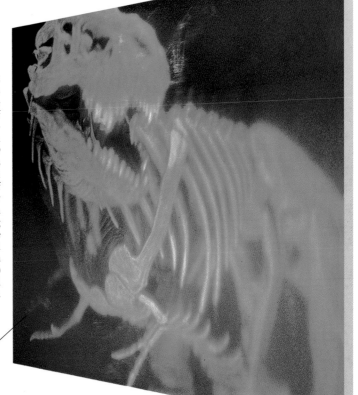

Hologram

Incoming light

Image

Eye

Eye traces back along light path

Reflected light is a replica of light produced by the object

REFLECTION HOLOGRAM
A reflection hologram is made by shining a reference beam and an object beam onto a thick film from opposite sides. The beams interfere to produce a pattern of light and dark on the film. When the hologram is viewed, this pattern reflects light in a way that produces a 3-D image of the original object.

COUNTERFEIT CRIME BUSTERS
In 1983, MasterCard was the first credit card company to print holograms on its cards to combat fraud. In 1984, *National Geographic* was the first major magazine to print a hologram on its front cover – it showed an American eagle. Today, holograms are all around us – often as a way of preventing counterfeiting, as on this "edge-to-edge" hologram CD, in which holographic images are part of the actual disc.

Full-color holograms embedded in CD

Digital cameras

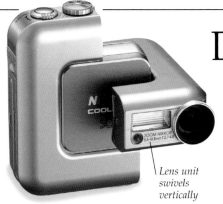

IT IS HARD TO BELIEVE THAT digital cameras have been available to consumers only since about 1996. Now, they outsell film cameras and, in time, seem likely to replace them. Their obvious advantage is that, because they do not use film, no processing is required. Pictures can be viewed immediately, either on the camera's own LCD screen or, after downloading to a computer, on a color monitor. They can be printed very quickly, too, either on a regular computer printer or by a professional photo laboratory. Instead of film, digital cameras have a light-sensitive imaging chip, or sensor, made up of millions of miniature picture elements called "pixels." This sensor has many advantages over film. Its sensitivity to light (or ISO rating) can even be altered from one picture to another – which until now could only be done by loading film of a different speed.

CUTTING-EDGE DESIGN
Freed from the need to worry about rolls of film, designers of digital cameras have come up with a wide variety of new designs. The lens unit on this Nikon Coolpix SQ swivels forward and backwards, making it easy to take pictures at unusual angles – from overhead, for example. When held at arm's length and pointed backward, it can even shoot self-portraits.

Lens unit swivels vertically

Shutter release button

Handgrip contains batteries and memory card

MEMORY CARDS
Each time a picture is taken, it is recorded on the camera's light-sensitive sensor. The camera's electronics translate the information it has acquired into the form of digital data, then transfers (or "writes") it to storage devices called memory cards. Decreasing in size almost as fast as they are increasing in capacity, these cards store the photographs until they can be downloaded from the camera to a computer or printer.

Loading a memory card into its camera slot

MemoryStick Pro

SD card

CompactFlash card

Microdrive

xD card

Lens hood minimizes flare

INSIDE A DIGITAL SLR CAMERA
Digital and film cameras work in very much the same way. They both have a variable-aperture lens that admits and focuses light, and they have a shutter that opens when the picture is taken. The major difference is that, in a digital camera, the light falls onto the surface of a light-sensitive sensor rather than onto unexposed film. In many digital cameras, the sensor is capable of capturing separate images or frames in such quick succession that it is possible to record short movie sequences. The cameras have built-in microphones, too, so the movies have sound.

PUTTING YOU IN THE PICTURE
This camera has both an electronic viewfinder (EVF) and a liquid crystal display (LCD). The EVF is a tiny, high-resolution color screen instead of the optical viewfinder found on most cameras. It is a through-the-lens design, so it can be used to preview exactly what will be recorded on the image sensor. The EVF and LCD screens can display images and the menu options for the camera controls.

Electronic viewfinder

Dial for setting exposure modes

LCD screen

Memory card slot

Pop-up flash

Mounting point (known as hot shoe) for external flash

Each sensor has its own filter

Color filter array

Green filter records green light

Color separation

HOW A PICTURE IS RECORDED
A digital image sensor is like a checkerboard or grid of tiny squares. Each square is a silicon photo diode that can record the brightness of the light falling on it when a picture is taken. But it can only "see" in tones of gray. In order to record color images, the diodes are alternately filtered so that some record red light, others green, and others blue. When the image is displayed, the combination of red, green, and blue in varying intensities recreates the colors of the original scene.

Electronic viewfinder

DRIVEN BY A CHIP
The light-sensitive sensor at the heart of every digital camera is likely to be a CCD (charge-coupled device) or a CMOS (complementary metal-oxide semiconductor). Both record an image that is then translated into digital data. The resolution of the chip is measured in megapixels – so this 8-megapixel camera, for example, has a chip that can capture images measuring 8 million pixels.

Controls for flash, metering, focusing, macro, and night-shooting

PIXELS AND FILM GRAIN
All digital images are made up of thousands of tiny blocks or pixels of color. Normally, the images are displayed at a size at which the human eye cannot detect them individually. But the image can be enlarged so that they become visible and the picture appears "pixelated." The higher the resolution of the image, the more it can be magnified before it breaks up. Film is similar – it is made up of tiny grains of silver halide and color dye that become visible when enlarged.

Film grain

Pixel structure

Photography in a digital world

Today, PHOTOGRAPHY HAS ONE FOOT firmly in the digital world, with the other likely to follow before long. After more than a century of depending on light-sensitive film, an increasing number of photographers are moving toward a digital future. There are many advantages. Digital cameras are easy to use, and produce photographs that can be viewed immediately. Digital photo files can be stored and used in many different ways – they can be downloaded onto a computer and used by software programs, sent to friends or family via email or phone, and posted on the Internet, for example. Moreover, images can be copied, corrected, resized, recolored, and manipulated in countless ways without loss of quality.

35-mm transparencies

35 mm negative strips

STORING PHOTOS
Digital-photo image files are stored on a memory card in the camera. When the card is full, pictures can be downloaded onto a computer. Large image files quickly fill a computer's hard disc, however, which is why they are usually transferred onto CD or DVD for storage.

Index print insert

USING A FILM SCANNER
A film scanner is used for turning negatives or transparencies into a form that a computer can understand. This is called "digitizing." The scanner shines light through a negative or transparency onto a digital image sensor similar to the ones in digital cameras. The sensor records the differences in brightness as electrical charges, then converts them to digital image data.

MAKING THE MOST OF SOFTWARE
Once images have been downloaded from the camera to the computer, software applications are used to display, sort, file, edit, and manipulate them. At their simplest, the programs will let you crop and resize pictures, organize them into albums, and make slideshows with them. But sophisticated packages like Adobe Photoshop give you access to the same tricks and special effects as the professionals (see p. 62).

LCD displays photos on camera's memory card

Photo management software

Mini tripod

Connection cable

DOWNLOADING IMAGES
There are two ways of downloading images from the camera's memory card to the computer. The camera can be directly connected to the computer using a cable (as shown here), or the card can be removed from the camera and inserted into a memory-card reader that has been connected to the computer.

Laptop computer

Flatbed scanner

HELPFUL GADGETS
Personal digital assistants (PDAs) are multipurpose handheld computers. They often act as cell phones, too, and can connect wirelessly to the Internet. It's no surprise that, like phones, they have digital cameras built in and can send photos to other phones or via email.

Portable digital photo album

CREATING PHOTO ALBUMS
Flatbed scanners are much like photocopiers. They can scan or digitize almost any image, from photographic prints, documents, and drawings to pages from books and magazines. Equipped with a transparency adapter, they will scan negatives and slides, too. You can even scan real objects – as long as they are small enough to fit on the bed of the scanner. It's a great way to convert items other than photos, such as flowers, toys, or coins, into digital files. Once digitized, they can be included in digital photo albums, digital scrapbooks, or school projects.

Old family photos ready to be scanned

MOBILE GALLERY
This palm-sized device is a portable multimedia player. It is essentially a computer hard drive with a small color screen. It can be used to download photos from memory cards, either for interim storage or to view them at a larger size than on the camera. When set to slideshow mode, it's ideal as a constantly changing "picture-frame" and for showing off photos to friends.

PRINTING PHOTOGRAPHS
Most digital photos are printed out at home on inkjet printers. When used with high-quality paper, they can produce very good results, especially if they have four, six, or more separate ink cartridges for different colors. For professional laboratory quality prints, you should choose a printer that uses ink ribbon rather than cartridges (like the one shown here). Many printers now print direct from memory cards – there is no need to download them to a computer first.

LCD screen for previewing print settings

Digital camera lens

Olympus P400 color printer

Single prints can be full-page or postcard size

FUN PICTURE MESSAGES
It's common now for a new cell phone to have a built-in digital camera. The quality of the pictures is still inferior to that of most digital cameras, but that's not the point. What makes camera phones such fun is that pictures can be sent to friends and family, from one phone to another, just an instant after they have been taken.

Cell phone displays digital photo

Photo trickery

CAN THE CAMERA LIE? Strictly speaking, no. It's a device that simply records an image of what's in front of it. However, in practice the answer is not so clear-cut. Photographers have always been able to influence a picture by controlling what the camera sees and what it doesn't – choosing a particular viewpoint, cropping out of the frame anything they do not want to appear, carefully selecting focus, exposure, and lighting. The tradition of manipulating pictures once they have been taken is known as "photo retouching" and it has long been an acknowledged skill. Nowadays, digital imaging has made the whole process easier. Anyone with a computer and suitable image-editing software can give it a try.

THAT'S THE SPIRIT
In the Victorian era, spirit photography became popular. The best-known spirit photographer was Frederick Hudson, who created this composite print showing the ghostly, underexposed image of a couple's deceased daughter. Many people at the time were convinced that such images were real.

FAIRY STORY
In 1917, two young girls, Frances Griffiths and Elsie Wright, produced photographs of themselves playing with fairies in their garden in Cottingley, Yorkshire. Experts declared the pictures genuine. More than 60 years later, in 1981, the pair finally admitted to the hoax and revealed that the paper fairies had been cut out of a book and pinned in place for the camera.

Trotsky stands next to Lenin

Lenin appears alone

BLURRING REALITY
On the computer, two photos can be combined by making them into separate "layers," then placing one on top of the other. The transparency of the top layer can be adjusted so that areas of the picture on the bottom layer can be seen through it. With some additional retouching, this is how this photographer blended a picture of his boots with the photo of his feet.

RETOUCHING HISTORY
In politics, those who have fallen from favor are often erased from official photographs, on the basis that if they no longer appear in the pictures, then history will forget them. Joseph Stalin had hundreds of photographs retouched to remove any traces of his enemies. This photograph was taken in 1919. Originally, it showed Vladimir Lenin (in the center) and Leon Trotsky (saluting) together at the second anniversary of the Russian Revolution. In a doctored version published in 1967, Trotsky has been airbrushed out.

Faked image using studio model of UFO

THEY CAME FROM SPACE
It has been estimated that there are more than 10,000 photographs claiming to be of unidentified flying objects (UFOs). Debate rages over whether they are genuine. The best fakes – whether products of traditional pen, ink, and airbrush or modern-day digital image-editing software – are skillfully done. They carefully match camera viewpoints, angles of view, and lighting quality and direction. Others, as here, are more openly created for fun.

Photo of boots forms top layer

MONSTERS AHOY!
Scotland's Loch Ness is the largest freshwater lake in Great Britain and is up to 750 ft (250 m) deep. It has long been rumored to be the home of "Nessie," a large, prehistoric creature. An early photograph of the monster was revealed to be a fake when one of the hoaxers made a deathbed confession at the age of 93. This picture was shot in 1977 by Anthony "Doc" Shiels, who claims that it is genuine.

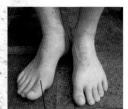

Photo of feet in same position forms second layer

The Loch Ness Monster?

One of 100 individual shots of groups of children

Top layer is made transparent so feet can be seen beneath boots

Final image after digital retouching

Empty church square forms background

NOT CHILD'S PLAY
This photograph is the joint effort of a professional photographer and a digital retoucher. It was commissioned by a French clothing company to show off its range of children's clothes in a single giant image. The photographer realized it would be impossible to get every child in the right pose at the right moment for a single camera exposure, so he shot 100 pictures of groups of them. The retoucher then placed each group digitally onto the background of the empty church square – all at very high resolution so that smaller areas could later be enlarged. The final digital image was composed of hundreds of different layers and took six days and nights to produce.

Did you know?

AMAZING FACTS

Nearly 85 billion photographs are taken every year worldwide – that's almost 2,700 every second.

Some 550 million households around the world own at least one film camera. And in the U.S., there is roughly one camera for every adult living in the country.

The first celebrity photographer was Frenchman Felix Nadar. He opened his first photographic studio in Paris in 1853 and became famous for his portraits of contemporary painters, novelists, and poets.

Julia Margaret Cameron is now regarded as one of the greatest 19th-century photographers, but she was not so well-respected at the time. Her pictures were often criticized for poor quality and shoddy presentation.

The very first Kodak camera, launched in 1888, contained a 20-ft (6-m) roll of light-sensitive paper – enough to produce 100 small circular pictures. But in 1914, the Tourist Multiple, patented by New Yorker Paul Dietz, outdid this. It held a 50-ft (15-m) roll of film – enough for more than 750 photos, or "a complete European tour," as its ads claimed.

Photography's popular 35-mm film format originally came from the film used in early movie cameras. Thomas Edison cut a roll of 70-mm Kodak film down the middle, producing two 35-mm-wide strips. He put perforated holes down the edges so they could be run through movie cameras and projectors. In 1924, Oscar Barnack also used 35-mm movie film for his prototype of what would become the Leica, the world's first commercially successful 35-mm camera.

The best place to store film is the refrigerator. The dyes stay colorfast for longer if film is kept in the dark at a low temperature.

A photograph by British artist Sam Taylor-Wood was draped around the outside of Selfridge's department store on London's Oxford Street in summer 2000. She claimed to be creating a modern-day version of the Elgin Marbles, a frieze of celebrities celebrating a temple of shopping. The photograph, called *XV Seconds*, measured 900 ft (300 m) by 60 ft (20 m).

The larger-than-life photograph *XV Seconds*

The "red eye" common in flash photographs is caused by the color of the blood vessels in the eye reflecting off the retina back into the camera lens.

The Japanese company Konica has developed an intelligent voice-activated camera. Called the Kanpai (*kanpai* means "cheers" in Japanese), it swivels on its built-in tripod and takes a snapshot whenever it hears a sound such as a burst of laughter or cheers.

A giant digital photomosaic comprising 39,000 different tiles and featuring self-portraits of 3,500 people was created by photographer Rankin and digital artist Robert Silvers, who invented the technique of making photomosaics. Called *You Can*, it was commissioned by Canon and was displayed wrapped around the IMAX movie theater in London in 2002. It measured 6,000 sq ft (2,000 sq m).

The Hubble Space Telescope uses digital cameras to take its astonishing photographs of deep space. Its postage stamp–sized imaging sensors are so sensitive to the faint light of distant galaxies that they can see objects a billion times fainter than the naked eye can see.

In December 2000, a Japanese photographer named Shinichi Yamamoto set the Guinness World Record for the longest photographic negative. It is 100 ft (30 m) long and 2.75 in (7 cm) wide. It shows a group of about 650 high-school students arranged in a circle around a homemade revolving panoramic camera. The camera rotated 13 times, capturing the students in 13 different poses on the same piece of film. The print from the negative is 476 ft (145 m) long.

What's in a name?

KODAK
George Eastman simply invented the word "Kodak." Although it doesn't mean anything, Eastman thought it was easy to remember and easy to pronounce in any language.

CANON
Canon cameras were originally called "Kwanons," after the Buddhist god of mercy, but the company switched to "Canon" to avoid upsetting religious groups.

FUJI
The company simply took its name from Japan's legendary Mount Fuji.

LEICA
The company started as Leitz in 1849, when it made lenses for microscopes and telescopes. When it switched to making cameras, it created the new name Leica from LEItz CAmera.

The giant digital mosaic, *You Can*, wrapped around London's Imax Cinema

Q Who invented photography?

A No single person can really be described as the inventor of photography. Instead, three men all working at about the same time can be said to have contributed to its discovery. They were Frenchmen Joseph Niépce and Louis Daguerre (see pp. 8–9), and Englishman William Henry Fox Talbot (see p. 10). They each devised a practical process for capturing a permanent photographic image. Credit should also go to George Eastman, the founder of Kodak, for bringing cameras and film to everyone.

Q Where did the term "photography" come from?

A It was first used in 1839 by John Herschel, a friend of Talbot. The word comes from the Greek words *photos* (light) and *graphos* (writing). Herschel also coined the terms "positive" and "negative."

Q How did early photographers get the correct exposure?

A Initially, the length of time an exposure was given was guesswork, arrived at largely by trial and error. Accuracy was not too important in the very early days because exposures often lasted several minutes. But as increasingly standardized photographic plates and film became more sensitive, exposures shortened and a more scientific method was required. The first exposure meters appeared in the 1880s. Photographers used them to time how long it took a small piece of photographic paper to darken when exposed to light. From this, they then calculated what shutter speed to use on the camera and what aperture to set on the lens.

Q Why are there so few early color photographs?

A Color photography was a much tougher problem to solve than black-and-white. In fact, the first photographic plates – even though they were designed for monochrome – could see only blue light. It was not until 1906 that panchromatic films were able to record red, green, and blue. Many of the earliest color photographs were in fact monochrome prints that were hand-tinted or painted. Color film is complex and is made up of multiple layers of emulsions, filters, and dyes. Color transparencies didn't arrive until 1936 and color negatives until 1950.

Q What type of camera was used to take the latest pictures of Mars?

A NASA's Mars Exploration Rover *Spirit* carries nine cameras altogether. Its Panoramic Camera, or "Pancam," takes photographs like the

Red dust covers landing cushions

Photo taken by NASA's *Spirit* of the lander that brought it to Mars

one shown here. It is a digital camera, of course, but somewhat surprisingly, it's only a one-megapixel model, which compares unfavorably with even the most inexpensive consumer cameras today. The difference is that its image sensor is much bigger, so each of the one million pixels it contains is about four times larger and more sensitive than normal.

Q Which is better quality – digital or film?

A Both are now comparable in quality. The real answer depends on the resolution of the digital image and the physical size of the negative or transparency. A high-resolution digital image taken with a 6-mega-pixel camera should produce as good a print as a 35-mm negative.

Record-Breakers

Prototype Phantom camera system (1946)

👁 OLDEST CAMERA
In 1816 Joseph Niépce devised his first "discovery" camera by adapting an existing camera obscura. He used it in his attempts to capture images on paper coated with light-sensitive silver chloride. Unfortunately, the images were very faint and they did not last. It was several more years before he found a way of making them permanent.

👁 OLDEST SURVIVING PHOTOGRAPH
The earliest known photograph that still survives today was taken by Joseph Niépce in 1826 or 1827 (see p. 8). Lost for decades, the "heliograph," as Niépce called it, was rediscovered by photo historian Helmut Gernsheim in 1952.

👁 MOST EXPENSIVE CAMERA
In January 2001, at Christie's in London, a unique camera fetched an auction price of £146,750 ($215,722). It was the prototype for a complete photographic system, called Phantom, designed in 1946 by the eccentric inventor, photographer, and English Member of Parliament Noel Pemberton Billing. The camera itself could be used not only to take pictures but also as a projector or enlarger. It came with an integrated kit that included developing tanks, units for storing film, paper, and batteries, and a contact printer. The camera never actually went into production.

👁 MOST EXPENSIVE PHOTOGRAPH
In May 2003, Christie's of London sold a 161-year-old photograph for a world-beating £565,250 ($893,095). It was called *Athènes* (1842) and showed the remains of the Athenian Temple of Olympian Zeus, or "Olympieion," on the Acropolis in Greece.

👁 LARGEST CAMERA
In 2003, the telescope on top of Hawaii's Mauna Kea was equipped with "Megacam," a French-built, 340-megapixel digital camera. The camera's field of view takes in four times as much sky as any other camera in the world. Its image sensor is capable of producing an image of more than one gigabyte in size.

Timeline

IT IS MORE THAN 165 YEARS SINCE Louis Daguerre and Henry Fox Talbot announced their rival photographic processes. During that time, photography has come a very long way – in part due to the ingenuity and perseverance of its many pioneers. However, in just the past 10 years or so, the introduction of digital cameras and digital image processing has brought about a period of extraordinary change in the world of photography.

Half-tone photograph of New York's shanty town, which appeared in the *New York Graphic* on March 4, 1880

Camera obscura projects image inside darkened room

1500–1700
Camera obscuras were equipped with simple lenses to focus images more sharply and make them brighter. From this time on, they were increasingly used by artists to help make accurate drawings.

1727
Johann Schulze, a Swiss professor of anatomy, accidentally discovered that silver compounds were photosensitive – that is, they changed color when exposed to light.

Image recorded on silver-coated copper plate

Framed daguerreotype studio portrait

1795
Thomas Wedgwood, son of the British potter Josiah, experimented with silhouette "sun prints" on light-sensitive leather coated with silver nitrate, but was unable to make the images permanent.

1826
In France, Joseph Niépce produced the world's first permanent camera image on a pewter plate coated with light-sensitive bitumen of Judea. It hardened where light fell on it. Any still soft after the exposure was washed off with lavender oil, leaving a permanent, recognizable image.

1839
Louis Daguerre's daguerreotype process was publicly announced. For the first time, there was a practical way of capturing, developing and fixing permanent photographic images, and a popular craze for studio portraiture took off.

1839
In England, Henry Fox Talbot announced his rival process. Unlike the daguerreotype, Talbot's calotype images were paper negatives, from which an unlimited number of positive prints could be made.

1851
Frederick Scott Archer invented the collodion process – a way of producing photo-sensitive glass plates that needed shorter exposure times and resulted in better images. Although still complex and cumbersome, cameras were now freed from the studio, and the first travel, documentary, and war photographs began to appear.

1861
James Clerk-Maxwell, a Scottish physicist, demonstrated the first color image, produced using red, green, and blue filters.

1871
The dry plate was invented and began to replace collodion wet plates. Slowly, photography was becoming easier and more accessible.

1877–78
Eadweard Muybridge's stop-motion photo sequences showed for the first time exactly how a horse's legs move at full gallop.

Lumière brothers

1880
The first halftone photograph was printed in a daily newspaper, the *New York Graphic*.

1888
George Eastman launched the first Kodak camera, and a mail-order processing and printing service.

1900
The first Kodak Brownie camera, loaded with flexible roll film, went on sale in the U.S. – at a widely affordable price of just $1.

1906
The first panchromatic film and plates went on sale. They were sensitive to blue, green, and red light – which improved the detail and range of tones in black-and-white photographs.

1907
The Lumière brothers in France introduced Autochrome plates – the first commercially available form of color photography.

1913
The Speed Graphic Press camera was launched in the U.S. It went on to become the standard camera for press photographers for the next 40 years.

1921
Man Ray and Moholy-Nagy produced photograms, images formed by placing objects on photographic paper and then exposing it to light.

1924
The German company Leitz introduced the Leica. It was the world's first successful 35-mm camera.

1932
Group f64 was formed by Ansel Adams, Edward Weston, and other photographers in the U.S. It promoted realistic photography as opposed to the soft-focus pictorial style that was popular at the time.

The first Leica in 1924 established the 35-mm format

1936
Kodachrome 35-mm color transparency film was introduced in the U.S. It was a "spinoff" from color film designed for movie cameras.

1942
Agfa and Kodacolor color-negative film was introduced, allowing low-cost color prints for the first time.

1947
The world's best-known photojournalistic picture agency, Magnum, was formed by Henri Cartier-Bresson, Robert Capa, David Seymour, and other photographers.

1947
Edwin Land introduced the first Polaroid camera, producing instant peel-apart black-and-white pictures.

Kodak Disc camera lasted for just four years

1949
The Contax S, made by the East German company Zeiss, was the first 35-mm SLR camera with a pentaprism viewfinder. It meant that the image the photographer saw was no longer reversed.

1959
The Nikon F 35-mm SLR marked the emergence of Japanese companies as major players in the photographic industry.

1963
Kodak launched the Instamatic. It used a new film format – the allegedly foolproof 126 "drop-in" cartridge.

1966
Antonioni's film *Blow Up* reflected the celebrity status of 1960s professional photographers.

1972
Kodak's compact 110 format film was designed for amateur pocket cameras.

1972
Polaroid launched the SX-70, a newly designed camera that took instant color photos on single sheets that no longer need peeling apart.

1976
The Canon AE-1 35-mm camera was the first to have a built-in microprocessor. Incorporating electronics reduced the number of camera parts by 300.

1981
The first photographs of Earth taken by the Shuttle astronauts were published.

1982
Sony demonstrated its prototype Mavica "still video" camera. It recorded images on floppy disks and played them back on a television set. "Mavica" was a contraction of MAgnetic VIdeo CAmera.

1983
The Kodak disc camera was launched. The format was not a success, and it was dropped in 1987.

1984
At the Los Angeles Olympics, Canon used a prototype color electronic still camera to take pictures and transmit them back to Japan over phone lines.

1990
The first version of Adobe Photoshop was launched for the Apple Macintosh. It has since become the standard software application for digital image manipulation.

1990
The first photographs taken by the Hubble Space Telescope were released.

David Hemmings in the classic 1966 movie *Blow Up*

1991
Kodak released the DCS-100 SLR digital camera. It was based on a Nikon body and lens, had an external disk drive and monitor, weighed 55 lb (25 kg), was carried in a small suitcase, and cost $30,000.

1992
Kodak launched PhotoCD, the first standard format for storing digital photographs on CD-ROM.

1996
Advanced Photo System (APS) was launched. Using filmstrips 24 mm wide instead of 35 mm, it was the first major new film format for 13 years.

1996
The first consumer digital cameras became widely available. Most were capable of taking pictures at only 640 x 480 pixels.

2000
Sharp released the first cell phone with a built-in digital camera.

2002
For the first time, annual sales of digital cameras overtook those of film cameras.

2003
Camera phones overtook the sales of digital cameras and camcorders combined.

Sharp J-SH04, the first camera cell phone

MUSÉE FRANÇAIS DE LA PHOTOGRAPHIE
This museum of photography is situated just south of Paris and was founded in 1960. It has a collection of about 35,000 items of photographic equipment that cover the entire history of photography – camera obscuras, prototype cameras, magic lanterns and projectors, 19th-century studio apparatus, and so on. It also has an estimated 1 million photographs – including many rare early daguerreotypes.

USEFUL WEBSITES

- Online exhibitions from Great Britain's National Museum of Photography, Film & Television:
  www.nmpft.org.uk
- Home of the George Eastman House, Rochester, New York:
  www.eastman.org
  Plus online exhibitions of items from the collection:
  www.geh.org
- A virtual museum of photography that exists only online:
  www.photographymuseum.com
- One of the largest photographic community sites:
  www.photo.net
- *National Geographic* magazine's photography site:
  www.nationalgeographic.com/photography
- Two sites devoted to the life and work of Joseph Niépce. One is based on a museum and research center at the house in which lived, in St-Loup-de-Varennes, France. Lots of information about early photographic processes:
  http://www.niepce.com
  The other is the website of the museum in Chalon-sur-Saône, France (see opposite):
  www.museeniepce.com
- Good source of information about digital cameras and digital imaging:
  www.dpreview.com
- Visible Earth – thousands of NASA satellite images of Earth:
  http://visibleearth.nasa.gov
- Excellent one-man site on the history of photography to 1920:
  www.rleggat.com/photohistory
- Website to accompany PBS TV series *American Photography: A Century of Images*: **www.pbs.org/ktca/americanphotography**
- Helios, online exhibitions from the Smithsonian American Art Museum:
  http://americanart.si.edu/collections/exhibits/helios

Find out more

ONE OF THE BEST WAYS to learn about photography is to develop the habit of looking carefully at every picture you see. Try to think what the photographer had in mind when he or she took it. What does it show? How has it been framed? What type of camera might have been used? What kind of lens? What is in and out of focus? Is it lit naturally or with flash? Have any special effects – digital or otherwise – been used? There are plenty of places to find photographs. Newspapers, magazines, and books are an obvious source, along with the Internet. And most countries have museums and galleries that regularly display the work of great photographers.

THE FOX TALBOT MUSEUM
Lacock Abbey in Wiltshire, England, was the home of Henry Fox Talbot, one of the pioneers of photography (see p. 10). In fact, the oldest surviving photographic negative is a photograph of one of the windows of the Abbey. It now houses a small museum where you can see examples of the "calotype" images he invented and a selection of his original photographic equipment, including the home-made "mousetrap" cameras with which he took some of the world's very first photographs.

Talbot's mousetrap camera (*c.* 1835)

SEASIDE CAMERA OBSCURA
Camera obscuras such as this one, on the pier at the English seaside resort of Eastbourne, have long been popular vacation attractions (see p. 6). The Eastbourne Camera Obscura was originally built in 1901, at which time it was the largest in Great Britain. After falling into disrepair for years, it was restored and reopened in 2003. A darkened circular room contains the viewing table on which an image captured by the lenses and mirror on top of the roof is projected. The whole roof revolves on enormous ball bearings.

Camera Obscura, Eastbourne Pier, England

NATIONAL MUSEUM OF PHOTOGRAPHY, FILM, AND TELEVISION

Since 1983, Great Britain's national collection of photography and moving pictures has been located in Bradford, England. The collection of cameras, photographic equipment, and works by leading photographers was started by the Science Museum in the 1880s and dates back to the birth of photography. The museum also covers film and TV. Interactive exhibits allow visitors to operate a TV camera, appear on screen, and try their hand at animation.

House built by George Eastman of Kodak

GEORGE EASTMAN HOUSE

Situated in Rochester, New York, the house and gardens were built by George Eastman, the founder of Kodak (see p. 18). After his death in 1932, the property deteriorated, but it was restored and opened as museum of photography and film in 1949. It has one of the world's largest collections of photographic and cinematographic equipment and an archive of photographs that includes over 400,000 negatives and prints by more than 8,000 photographers.

Experiment with unusual camera angles and viewpoints

MUSÉE NICÉPHORE NIÉPCE

Chalon-sur-Saône, south of Dijon in France, was the birthplace of Joseph Nicéphore Niépce, one of the inventors of photography (see p. 8). It is now the home of one of France's most important museums of the history of photography, with displays detailing such early photographic processes and techniques as heliographs, calotypes, daguerreotypes, collodion, Autochrome, and many more.

Niépce's statue in Chalon-sur-Saône, France

A
NICEPHORE NIEPCE
INVENTEVR DE LA PHOTOGRAPHIE
NE A CHALON S.S. LE 7 MARS 1765

ENROLL IN A PHOTOGRAPHY COURSE

There is no better way of getting to grips with how photography works than by taking pictures yourself. Joining a local camera club or taking a photography course will put you in contact with photographers willing to share their experience and help you learn. Do not be afraid to experiment. Look for unusual subjects and viewpoints, and try different compositions and exposure settings. With digital cameras, there is no film to waste – if you are not happy with a picture, just delete it and take another one!

Places to visit

METROPOLITAN MUSEUM OF ART, NEW YORK
www.metmuseum.org
Collection of more than 15,000 works, mostly from Europe and the U.S. Highlights include:
• Rubel Collection – examples of early British photography, including a rare album of photographs by Henry Fox Talbot
• Alfred Stieglitz Collection – pictorialist photography.

CALIFORNIA MUSEUM OF PHOTOGRAPHY
www.cmp.ucr.edu
Affiliated with University of California, Riverside. Exhibitions plus digital studio. Look for:
• Bingham Technology Collection – 10,000 cameras and viewing devices.
• World's largest collection of vintage stereographs.

MUSEUM OF CONTEMPORARY PHOTOGRAPHY, CHICAGO
www.mocp.org
Specializes in the work of American photographers.

MUSEUM OF PHOTOGRAPHIC ARTS, SAN DIEGO
www.mopa.org
Collection of both historical and contemporary photographs.

PHOTOGRAPHER'S GALLERY, LONDON, ENGLAND
www.photonet.org.uk
Exhibits work by contemporary and emerging photographers as well as established names.

NATIONAL PORTRAIT GALLERY, LONDON, ENGLAND
www.npg.org.uk
Collection of more than 160,000 photographs and exhibitions of works from the past and present.

CENTRE NATIONAL DE LA PHOTOGRAPHIE, PARIS, FRANCE
www.cnp-photographie.com
Exhibitions of contemporary photography, digital photos, and video imagery.

Glossary

Autochrome of a couple having tea in the garden in about 1910.

APERTURE The hole that controls how much light passes through a lens. It can be widened to let in more light and narrowed to admit less. The size of the aperture is measured in f numbers or f stops. It also affects depth of field.

ASA Rating for film speed devised by the American Standards Association. Now generally replaced by ISO.

AUTOCHROME A method of producing color transparencies, invented by the Lumière brothers. Black-and-white film was coated with tiny grains of starch dyed red, green, and blue. The starch grains act as color filters to create the optical effect of a colored image.

BITMAP An image made up of a pattern or "map" of pixels, each of which has its own color and tone.

CALOTYPE The first negative/positive process, invented by Fox Talbot. The negatives were thin sheets of translucent paper made light-sensitive by coating them with silver iodide solution. Positive images were contact-printed from them.

CCD Charge Coupled Device – an array of sensors in a digital camera or scanner that creates a digitized image. In high-resolution devices, CMOS (Complementary Metal Oxide Semiconductor) sensors may be used.

COLLODION Nitrated cotton (gun-cotton) dissolved in a mixture of ether and alcohol, used to bind light-sensitive silver halides to so-called "wet" glass photographic plates. The process was invented by Frederick Scott Archer in 1851.

COLOR TEMPERATURE A measure of the color quality of a light source, expressed in Kelvins. Warm golden light at dusk, for example, has a lower color temperature than daylight at noon.

CONTACT PRINTING Making same-size prints by exposing printing paper to light while in direct contact with negatives.

DAGUERREOTYPE An image created on a silver-plated copper sheet coated with light-sensitive silver iodide. The process was invented by Louis Daguerre in 1839.

DEPTH OF FIELD The distance between the nearest and farthest point from the camera within which a subject is in sharp focus. Depth of field is dependent on the aperture setting and focal length of the lens. A wide aperture at a long focal length gives a shallow depth of field.

DEVELOPER The chemical used to treat exposed film or photographic paper so that invisible images recorded by the light-sensitive material become visible.

DIGITIZE To create a digital image by converting color and brightness values into binary form.

DRY PLATE The gelatin-coated photographic plates first manufactured by Richard Leach Maddox in 1878. They replaced wet collodion plates.

EMULSION A mixture of light-sensitive compounds and gelatin put on various bases to make film and printing papers.

EXPOSURE METER A device for measuring the amount of light falling on, or being reflected by, a subject. It is used to calculate the aperture and shutter speed that will give a correct exposure.

FILE FORMAT The form in which a digital image is stored and handled. Common file formats for digital photography are JPEG, TIFF, and RAW.

Image taken with a fisheye lens

FILTER Transparent lens attachment that modifies light passing through it – coloring or polarizing it, for example.

FISHEYE LENS Extreme wide-angle lens, sometimes with a view of 180 degrees or more.

FIXER The chemical used to stabilize light-sensitive film or paper so that it no longer reacts to light. Fixing agent is still sometimes called "hypo" (hyposulfite of soda or sodium thiosulfate).

FLASH SYNCHRONIZATION Method of timing the maximum light output of a flash to coincide with the moment that the camera's shutter is fully open.

F NUMBERS A system for indicating aperture. The f number is equivalent to the focal length of the lens divided by the effective diameter of the aperture. The lower the f number, the wider the aperture.

FOCAL LENGTH The focal length of a lens determines its angle of view. A wide-angle lens has a wide angle of view and is able to capture an image of much of the scene in front of it. A telephoto lens has a narrow angle of view and captures an image of only a small area but magnifies it, like a telescope. Wide-angle lenses have short focal lengths, and telephoto lenses have long focal lengths. Focal length is measured in millimeters.

FOCUS The point at which light rays passing through a lens converge to give a clear and sharply defined image of a subject.

GRAIN Tiny particles of black metallic silver, irregularly clumped together, that are formed when film is developed. They make up the image. The finer the grain, the less visible the individual particles are to the eye.

Black-and-white contact sheet

HALF-TONE A book and newspaper printing process that uses patterns of tiny dots of different sizes to reproduce the gradations in tone of a photographic image.

HOLOGRAM A three-dimensional (3-D) image that is created using laser light.

HOT SHOE The fitting on top of a camera that holds a flashgun. The hot shoe contains electrical connections that automatically synchronize the flash with the shutter.

INCIDENT LIGHT The light that falls on a subject, as opposed to the light reflected by it. Used by some exposure meters.

ISO Rating for the sensitivity or "speed" of film devised by the International Standards Organization. Also used to indicate sensitivity settings on digital image sensors.

LARGE-FORMAT CAMERA General term for cameras taking pictures 5 x 4 in (12.5 x 10 cm) and larger.

LENS A transparent glass disc with at least one curved surface. Rays of light that pass through a lens are bent, causing them to converge or diverge. A camera lens is usually made up of a number of separate lenses or groups of lens elements, which can be adjusted to bring an image into sharp focus on the surface of the film or digital image sensor.

MACRO Extreme close-up photography, producing images life-size or up to a magnification of about x 10, is called macrophotography.

MONTAGE Composite picture made from a number of images.

MEGAPIXEL One million pixels.

MEMORY CARD Removable storage medium for digital images – sometimes called "digital film."

NEGATIVE A negative is produced by developing exposed film. It carries a transparent image of the scene that has been photographed but one in which tones and colors are reversed: dark areas become light, and light areas become dark. When light is shined through a negative onto photographic paper, a positive print is produced.

PENTAPRISM Five-sided glass prism added to SLR cameras to show the view through the lens upright and the right way around.

PHOTOMICROGRAPHY Taking pictures through a microscope.

PINHOLE CAMERA A simple camera that uses a very small hole instead of a lens.

PIXEL Abbreviation for "picture element," the smallest unit of color and tone in a digital image. Each pixel has a value specifying its own color and tone. It displays as a single square of light on a computer monitor.

PLATE CAMERA Camera originally designed to take glass plates or large-format sheets of film.

POLARIZING FILTER Colorless filter able to absorb certain kinds of light. Used for intensifying the blue of skies and reducing reflections in water and glass.

1950s Micro-Press plate camera

RANGEFINDER A camera focusing system that determines the distance between camera and subject. The subject is viewed simultaneously from two positions a short distance apart, showing two images that are then matched or lined up. This adjustment is usually linked or "coupled" to the focusing mechanism of the camera lens.

RED EYE Effect in which flash causes the pupils of a subject's eyes to appear red instead of black. Caused when translucent blood in the retina at the back of the eye reflects red light into the camera.

Photomicrograph of a fruit fly

RESOLUTION The degree of detail in a digital image. Measured by the number of pixels per inch (ppi) or dots per inch (dpi).

RGB Red, Green, Blue; the three primary colors used to produce full-color images on television screens and computer monitors. Equal proportions of red, green, and blue produce white. Mixed in varying proportions, they can produce all the colors of the spectrum.

SCANNER A device for creating digitized image files from print, negative, transparency, or even 3-D originals.

SHUTTER Mechanism for controlling the time that light is allowed to act on the film or digital image sensor in a camera.

SLR A single-lens reflex (SLR) camera allows the user to preview the image through the picture-taking lens itself. It uses a hinged mirror between the lens and the film to divert an image into the viewfinder.

SPEED Sensitivity to light.

STOP In the darkroom, the chemical "stop" bath halts the development process by neutralizing the developer. F numbers are also known as f stops.

TELEPHOTO A lens with a long focal length, used for enlarging distant subjects.

TRANSPARENCY A positive image on transparent film. The opposite of a negative.

TLR A twin-lens reflex (TLR) camera has two lenses of identical focal length. The viewfinder lens forms an image on the focusing screen, the picture-taking lens focuses the image on the film plane.

VIEWFINDER The device through which you look when framing or composing a photograph. It sometimes features an optical mechanism (such as a split screen) that helps with manual focusing. The viewfinder often also displays information about the camera's exposure settings.

VIGNETTING Imaging technique in which the edges of the picture are gradually faded to black or white. It can also be an optical effect caused by a lens, lens attachment, or obstruction.

WIDE-ANGLE LENS A lens with a short focal length and a wide angle of view.

ZOOM LENS A lens with a variable focal length that can be adjusted from wide-angle to telephoto settings.

Index
ABC

Acknowledgments

Cooling Brown would like to thank: Peter Cooling and Steve Jones for illustrations. Andy Crawford for photography. Alistair King and Evelynne Stoikou for modelling. Katherine Hinton, Alasdair Greenyer and Sarah Goodwin at The National Bird of Prey Centre, Newent Gloucestershire, UK. Andy Pepper for his holographic expertise.

Index Hilary Bird

The publisher would like to thank the following for their kind permission to reproduce their photographs:

a=above; b=below; c=center; l=left; r=right; t=top

akg-images: 6tr, 6cl, 21tl; Paul Almasy 23bl. **Alamy Images:** Adrian Chinery 68b; ImageState/Dan Burton 49tl; Jennifer Weinberg 23br; Joe Sohm 71tr; Philip Lewis 70-71; Phototake Inc/Michael Covington 46crb; Stephen Frink Collection 49b. **Louise Ang:** 39b. **The Art Archive:** Tate Gallery London/Eileen Tweedy 16bl. **Associated Press AP:** Koji Sasahara 55bl. **Cris Benton:** 45crb, 45bc. **Bridgeman Art Library:** Haags Gemeentemuseum. Netherlands 17br; Musee d'Orsay, Paris, France 16cr; Musee des Beaux Arts, Pau, France/Giraudon 17cl; Museum of Fine Arts, Houston, Texas, USA/Brown Foundation Accessions Endowment Fund 17tl; Private Collection/Julian Hartnoll, London, UK 7t; Private Collection/Peter Willi 17tr; Science Museum, London, UK 8cr, 18c. **Canon (UK) Ltd:** 50c, 51cal. **Christie's Images Ltd:** 65tr. **Corbis:** Alinari Archives 12-13bc; Andrew

Cowie/Colorsport 27clb; Anthony Redpath 31tr; B. Bisson/PH. Caron/Sygma 26bl; Bettmann 6cr, 8cla, 9br, 15c, 27tr, 30tr, 30bl, 41tr, 44tl; Bob Krist 44br, 48bl; David Roseburg 31c; David Turnley 41b; Dorothea Lange 40tl; Eadweard Muybridge 34c; Hulton-Deutsch Collection 16tl, 19tr; James A. Sugar 43bl; Jeffrey L. Rotman 48cr; Jim Reed 43c; Joe McBride 42-43; Kennan Ward 50bl; Massimo Listri 32cl; Paul Almasy 22cr; Peter M. Fisher 61br; Stapleton Collection 16cl; Tim McGuire 42tl; Todd A. Gipstein 69br. **Digital Mapping Camera (DMC®)** image courtesy of Intergraph Corporation: 44bc. **DK Images:** © Judith Miller/DK/Law Fine Art Limited, Berkshire 62tl (frame); Dinesh Khanna 65tr; H. Keith Melton Collection 2bl, 4tr, 54tr, 54cr, 54tl, 54bl, 54br, 54cbl, 55cl, 55br, 55tl, 55tr, 55cal; Imperial War Museum 55cr, 55crb; Observatory Museum, part of the Albany Museum complex, Grahamstown, South Africa 7br; Rare Camera Company 31tl; Science Museum 4tl, 4cr, 8clb, 11tr, 11cal, 56cl, 56c, 56crb, 56cll, 56cr (mirror), 57cl; Stephen Oliver 32tr. **George Eastman House:** 15tl, 26tl; Barbara Galasso 69c. **Epson:** 61tl. **Mary Evans Picture Library:** 9cra, 62tl. **Fortean Picture Library:** 62cl, 63cl, 63cr. **John Frost Historical Newspapers:** 41c, 66tr. **Fujifilm UK:** 5tr, 30cb, 58cb. **Getty Images:** Aaron Strong 27bc; Bob Elsdale 35tr; Kim Heacox 42br; Mark Segal 38-39c; Peter David 49tr; Time Life Pictures 23t. **Hulton Archive/Getty Images:** 8tl; A H Robinson 39tl; Archive Photos 21b; Fox Photos 18br; London Express 14bl; Otto Herschan 14bcl; Picture Post 20bc; Three Lions 12tr, 22cl. **Barry Jackson:** 62-63bl, 63ca, 63c. **David King Collection:** 62clb, 62br. **Kobal Collection:** MGM 67tr. **Kodak:** 19br. **Lexar**

Media: 58c, 58cbl. **Woody Mayhew – Nexus America:** 2c, 48bc. **Microtek:** 60tr. **Musée Français de la Photographie:** Département de l'Essonne, Bièvres, France. Photo Remi Calzada 68tl. **N.H.P.A.:** Andy Rouse 50bc; B & C Alexander 26cr; John Shaw 50cr; Kevin Schafer 50tr; Stephen Dalton 51cal. **NASA:** 45c, 45cbl. **National Geographic Image Collection:** Bobby Model 42tl. **National Museum of Photography, Film and Television:** 69t. **Network Photographers:** Robert Doisneau/Rapho/Network Photographers 22ca. **Nikon:** 2bcl, 22crb, 26cb, 26br, 58tl, 59cr. **John Offenbach:** Photography by John Offenbach. Agency: BETC Euro/RSCG Paris. Client: Petit Bateau 63cb, 63br, 63bl. **Olympus:** 58bcl, 61c. **palmOne:** 61tr. **Panoramic Images:** Vladpans 38bl. **Photo-Me International Plc:** 31tcr. **Harry Ransom Humanities Research Center, The University of Texas at Austin:** 16-17bc. **Reuters:** 53bl, 57tl; Goran Tomasevic AS/CRB IRAQ BAGHDAD 41tl; Mario Laporta/CRB Italy Volcano Catania 43bc. **Rex Features:** Alexander Caminada (ACM) 57br; Nils Jorgensen 64tr, 64bl; RYB 40bc; Sipa Press 45tl, 45cla; SWD 43tc. **Rollei:** 27c. **Royal Astronomical Society Library:** 46cl. **Science & Society Picture Library:** National Museum of Photography, Film and Television 4crb, 8-9b, 9tl, 10bl, 10bcl, 11br, 12cl, 12bl, 12bcl, 13c, 13cbr, 13cr, 14cl, 14c, 14-15c, 15tr, 15tc, 15br, 18tl, 18bl, 18cbl, 19tc, 19cla, 19c, 20cl, 20cr, 21tr, 22tl, 22cb, 22cbl, 30cl, 34clb, 34-35tc, 38tl, 39tr, 56clb, 56bc, 66c, 67cl, 67bl, 68cr, 71cr; Science Museum 6cb, 7cr, 7l, 10cl, 13tr, 13cra, 14tr, 34tl, 34cra, 40tl, 44tl, 47tl, 47tcl, 53tr, 53cr, 57tr, 58bl, 60c, 61bc, 66cl, 66bl. **Science Photo Library:** 48tl; Aerofilms Ltd 44c; Alfred Pasieka 53c; Anthony

Mercieca 35c; Astrid & Hanns-Frieder Michler 36br; Biophoto Associates 36cb; Claude Nuridsany & Marie Perennou 53tl, 53tcl; Colin Cuthbert 57tr; Darwin Dale 36cr; Eye of Science 71bl; Gusto 52tl; Jerry Wachter 34-35bc; Mehau Kulyk 52cbr; NASA 46bl; NASA/JPL/Cornell 65cl; National Cancer Institute 37tcr; Philippe Plailly/Eurelios 37tl; Planetary Visions Ltd 45tr; Professor Harold Edgerton 35tl; Sovereign, ISM 52bl; Space Telescope Science Institute 66-67; Space Telescope Science Institute/NASA 47b; University of Cambridge Collection of Aerial Photographs 52bl; Volker Steger 37cr; VVG 37b, 37car. **Seitz Phototechnik AG/Switzerland:** 38br. **Sharp Corporation, Japan** 67br. **Sigma Imaging (UK) Ltd:** 27br. **SmartDisk:** 61cra. **Sony United Kingdom Limited:** 2cra, 2br, 58-59c, 59tc; **Topfoto.co.uk:** 12tr, 14br, 18-19c, 36tl; NMPFT, Bradford/HIP 10tr, 10cb, 11b, 70tl; Science Museum, London/HIP 11tl. **www.UnderwaterPhotography.com:** 48cl. **Roger Viollet:** 40cr. **Wildlife Watching Supplies:** Kevin Keatley 50cl. **Jack and Beverley Wilgus:** 6bl.

Jacket credits: Front: © Superstock (r); © Stuart Westmorland/CORBIS (l); top, l-r: © Science Museum; © Bridgman Art Library, London/ New York: Science Museum; Image Courtesy of Aquatica. Back: © National Museum of Photography, Film, and Television (tr); © Science Museum (cr).

All other images © Dorling Kindersley

For further information see: www.dkimages.com